The Art of Being Well Informed

Andrew P. Garvin

WITH ROBERT BERKMAN

Avery Publishing Group

Garden City Park, New York

Cover Designer: Ann Vestal
Editors: Vanessa Elder and Elaine Will Sparber
Typesetter: Bonnie Freid
Printer: Paragon Press, Honesdale, PA

Cataloging-in-Publication Data

Garvin, Andrew P.
   The art of being well informed: what you need to know to gain
   the winning edge in business / Andrew P. Garvin with Robert
   Berkman.—Rev. ed.
      p.; cm.
      Includes bibliographical references and index.
      ISBN 0-89529-730-2

   1. Communication in management. 2. Industry—United States—
Information services. 3. Information services—Guidebooks. 4.
Data bases—Guidebooks. 5. Internet (Computer network) I.
Berkman, Robert I. II. Title.

HF5718.G37 1996   658.4′5
                                                   QB196-30054

Printed in the United States of America

10   9   8   7   6   5   4   3   2   1

Contents

To Linda, Kira, and Jeffrey

CREDITS

Acknowledgments

I wish to express my sincere thanks to all the dedicated professional people who have worked for and with me in the knowledge business throughout the past twenty years. Without them, this book would not have been possible. In particular, special contributions were made by Kathleen Bingham, Anne Dennis, Elke Kastner, Neal McIlvane, Tom Miller, and Frances Spigai.

Hubert Bermont and Robert Berkman provided much of the inspiration and the behind-the-scenes effort that helped make my concepts readable.

My thanks, also, to the staff of FIND/SVP and to the many individuals who provided comments and suggestions to help make this revised edition as up-to-date as possible.

—Andrew P. Garvin

Preface

Some years ago, a friend of mine called me in a panic. He was desperate. "My ten-week-old daughter has just been diagnosed with an apparently rare disease I can't even pronounce," he said. "She may die. The pediatrician has never even encountered a case before.":

"How can I help?" I asked.

"I need to find out about this condition..I must find the best care...I must save her life!" he yelled.

Fortunately, since 1969 I've headed FIND/SVP, a company that helps business people find out what they need to know. I applied the same principles used in my business to help my friend.

After getting the correct spelling of his daughter's condition—"sub-glottic hemangioma"—we discovered in various medical textbooks, like the *Merck Manual* and *Current Therapy*, that it was very rare, especially in children so young.

"Now what?" my friend asked, "I want the greatest expert in the field to treat her!"

After I calmed him down, we proceeded with a step-by-step investigation. First, I suggested we find out as much as we could about the condition by reading everything that's been published about it. Some of the consultants and researchers at FIND/SVP helped by searching computer databases like *Health Periodicals Database* and *Medline*. Others suggested the databases offered by the National Organization for Rare Disorders. Through these, we found references to articles about the disease and treatment all the way back to 1966. We obtained the articles using a variety of firms that specialized in obtaining hard-to-find articles from medical journals and the like.

Within a day, my friend was a lay-expert on sub-glottic hemangiomas in children. By poring over the articles carefully, he unearthed names of doctors who specialize in this field. Four names kept coming up—two in the United States, one in Canada, and one in London. My friend called all of them and, armed with plenty of knowledge from his reading, was able to intelligently interview them. Finally, he picked one in Cincinnati. He flew his daughter there on a special medical plan, and an operation was quickly performed.

Happily, the little girl's life was saved.

I tell this story because it demonstrates how important it is to know how to become well informed. Sometimes it truly is a matter of life and death.

Most of the time, however, being well informed simply helps us to succeed at things we must do every day: solve problems, make business decisions, and explore opportunities.

Being well informed means having the right information and knowledge at the right time (and at the right price). The need to know—and to know quickly—is a key factor dominating our business and personal lives. Never before in history has there been so much information so readily available, but most of us have so little time to find it. We're too busy. Decisions have to be made too quickly. Just think about how the fax machine sped up the pace of business in only a few years.

Now, in the mid-nineties, new developments like E-mail and the Internet are speeding up the pace even more, while simultaneously creating an even bigger information explosion. If my friend called today with the same problem, we'd have far more medical databases to consult, we'd be searching for doctors and experts worldwide via the Internet, and sharing experiences and information about sub-glottic hemangiomas through online discussion groups and forums.

To compete effectively, we need to be continuously informed. Yet it always amazes me to see how few of my friends and business acquaintances really know how to find information—how to get smart fast about a new subject—or even how to ask the right questions in order to get the right answers.

Actually, it shouldn't be surprising, since finding information is not really taught in school or in college. Where do you learn that asking someone , "Do you have any information on..." is not nearly as effective as asking "Who is the best person to ask for information on..."?

The purpose of this book is to help you ask better questions so you get better answers, and to acquaint you with all the aspects of today's information environment so you can benefit from it.

Chapter 1 describes why information is the key to success. Chapter 2 explains why it's so dangerous to make assumptions, and looks at the need for solid and reliable data. In Chapter 3, you'll learn how to formulate good questions—questions that will get you the answers you need to efficiently solve problems. Chapter 4 delineates the actual costs of the different types of information, and explains how you can determined what a particular piece of information is worth to you. Chapter 5 explains how to judge the quality of the information you get, and outlines the pitfalls of various information sources. In Chapter 6, you'll find a detailed examination of our information environment, including a look at new and future resources. Chapter 7 describes the world of online databases, and provides actual examples of database searches. The new Internet phenomenon—a revolutionary development since the last edition of this book—and it's significance to you is covered in Chapter 8.

"Information paralysis" is an all-too-common problem in today's world. Chapter 9 examines this peculiar disease, and discusses how it can be cured. Chapter 10 describes how to create your own information-finding system Finally, Chapter 11 pulls everything together by providing a unique step-by-step guide to assembling an information report. Key listings of important information sources, databases, information-finding companies and how-to-books can be found in the appendices.

One word of caution: while the tips and techniques described in this book have generally stood the test of time, the specific information sources are changing rapidly. This is especially true of the Internet. So consider any examples we use as indicators, not guaranteed up-to-date sources.

Knowing how to be well informed is something of an art. I hope you'll learn a little of it from this book.

Andrew P. Garvin
President
FIND/SVP, Inc.
New York, NY

Introduction

The most important thing for business and professional people to have is often the most difficult thing for them to find: information. Information can make the difference between a decision and a guess, between success and failure, between wealth and poverty.

As the saying goes, knowledge is power. The ability to make successful decisions, depends directly upon the amount of knowledge you have. Knowledge results from information. How you can become the kind of individual who can acquire valuable information quickly, easily, and economically is the subject of this book.

Books are published in spates. When a subject is hot, a number of publishers jump into the fray with pertinent titles, but all the books tend to say the same thing. The subject of information remains one of the hottest. However, we have no intention of repeating what the others are saying. There are many fine books available that will tell you all about hundreds and hundreds of valuable sources of information. Among the most notable of these is Lorna Daniells' Business Information Sources (3rd Edition, University of California Press, 1993). This is no such source book, although we do mention and list a number of the best sources in the text and in the appendixes.

There are also many how-to books out there that explain, usually in technical terms, how to perform market research. These will tell you about the different kinds of research, about designing surveys, and performing tabulations, and about a great variety of techniques that the average executive doesn't want to be bothered with. Some of the best of these how-to books are listed in the appendix. Our book is not a how-to book either, although we will try to tell you something about how to be an effective information-gatherer.

This book deals specifically with raising your "information consciousness." Until this consciousness is enhanced, all the source books and how-to books in the world will be of little value to you.

Raising your information consciousness means learning how to think in ways that result in your being well informed, in being infinitely more resourceful than you are now. This is not easy, but it is far easier than solving problems in, say, nuclear physics.

Being well informed takes time, effort, curiosity, and some thought. You have to be able to ask the right questions and to understand how the right answers may be found. If you can find the right information, you can use it. Clearly, the more you know about something, the better you can control your own situation. Knowledge is a synthesis of information. And knowing means winning.

Many people have no idea how to find what they need to know. This surprised us when we first researched this book in the early 1980s and surprised us even more when we first revised the book in 1993. Now, at the end of 1995, we find this state of affairs to be downright embarrassing, especially when you consider the enormous amount of hype and popular media coverage of information online and the Internet. The fact remains, the majority of U.S. business people are still mostly in the dark when it comes to figuring out where to go to find a basic piece of information: whether it be a company financial, an industry overview, a product analysis, or any other piece of business information that is readily available—often instantly and at very low cost—for those with just a little bit of information knowledge.

But although we are still dismayed at how little people know about finding information, we are also more understanding as to why this may be the case, and what creates such a lack of information know-how among U.S. businesspersons. We believe there are several causes:

1. Lack of cultural support for the value of information. In the U.S. information is not valued as highly as it is in some other cultures. In Japan, for example, there are reportedly lines to get into the company library. And inside the library, CEOs sit at tables reading though annual reports of their competitors!

2. Information paralysis. As more and more information has become available, and choices for access increase, it can become more difficult to figure out where to go to do research. Should you first check the library card catalog, a printed index, a CD-ROM, America Online, CompuServe, your firm's online news delivery network, or the Internet? Some have just thrown up their hands, frustrated, and given up.

3. No obvious connection to one's job. It's not always clear to business people what the connection is between being able to effectively find and use information and how well they carry out their job duties. We hope reading this book makes that connection a lot clearer.

4. Lack of information education. Although we live in the information age, there are few, if any, degrees or educational programs that concentrate on teaching people how to find, use and understand information. The only officially recognized degree program is the Masters of Library Science (MLS) degree; however, courses in this field have been narrowly focused to meet the needs of traditional librarians. Over the last few years, though, we have finally seen the creation of some good courses in information access, which are often connected to a program in business, journalism, or communications.

Luckily, you do not have to be held hostage to these circumstances. While this book cannot solve all these problems, we are confident that you can make a quantum leap in your information consciousness and jump ahead of the pack. So though there will still always be those who, no matter what the state of technology and knowledge, are unsure how to find and use information, you will. And that, we believe, will make the difference between success and mediocrity.

Don't just take our word for it either! Tom Peters has said that "knowledge is the only sustainable competitive advantage" available to companies today. And according to futurist and writer Alvin Toffler, we are all today living in what he calls a "knowledge economy." C.K. Prahalad, author of *Competing for the Future*, Ernst & Young's Thomas Davenport and others agree that the obtaining, measuring, and leveraging of knowledge will be the key to success for businesses who want to survive and succeed in the 1990s. We'll talk more about this in Chapter 1.

Not everyone is in the dark, of course, when it comes to understanding information. There do exist some enlightened business people who have developed a high degree of what we call "information consciousness." We have found that these people have some of the same characteristics:

- They tend to read a lot
- They keep lots of files on all kinds of things
- They have an insatiable curiosity
- They prefer authoritative opinion to gossip
- They can quickly translate problems into information questions
- They like information in all formats—print, broadcast, and online

In short, these people enjoy a high degree of information literacy. We all know about and have been exposed to Intelligence Quotients all our lives. But these people have developed a very high Information Quotient. There is, of course, no such thing as an Information Quotient test yet, because no one has developed one. Perhaps someday we will.

What about that information explosion?

Information Overload

Today's businessperson is up to his or her eyeballs in internal e-mail messages, faxes, office memos, magazine subscriptions, voice mail, regular mail—and for some—Internet e-mail and news group messages on top of that.

As you scramble to try to manage this torrent of information, your frustrations mount. There's just no time you say to deal with all of this stuff! How can I get any real work done if I have to figure out what to do with all of this. And what happened to that supposed paperless office anyway? (It's just about to emerge along with household robot workers and jet pack flying).

What's going on? Why are we all swimming in paper, and spending hours trying to keep up with electronic information as well? It's not just because there are more sources of information: the number of business information sources has been growing for decades. What is new (and by new we can say beginning around the early 1980s and continuing through today) is this:

1. the microchip revolution: responsible for PCs, fax machines, e-mail, networks, phone-mail and the Internet. This technology has made it fast and easy to both create and disseminate information.

2. the emergence of the global economy and the increased level of competition it has brought to all business;

3. the effect of the combination of these first two factors which have placed a premium on increasing speed and lowering costs to remain competitive;

4. the move to reduce staff as the primary means of lowering costs. With fewer people around (especially secretaries, who

served as human information filters) there's just more work to be done by the people that are left;

5. replacing some of the activities of laid off people with technology, which again speeds up the pace of business and facilitates information creation and dissemination. According to Fortune magazine, since 1987, U.S. businesses have added over 130 million information receptacles in what the magazine calls the current "Infobog."

The result? A frantic battle by downsized, overworked staffs to stay on top of a seemingly never-ending deluge of data from e-mail, phone mail, faxes, databases, Internet news groups, regular mail, and who knows what else coming down the pipe next! Says Michel Bauwens, a futurist and information professional who created a one person "virtual library" for BP Nutrition in Antwerp, Belgium, "whereas before the right information wasn't available and lots of efforts had to be duplicated, it now sometimes seems that more time is spent digesting information than actually acting on it. "

The near term future doesn't look any more promising. Sure there are lots of proposed technological solutions. There's the crop of new "PDAs": Personal Digital Assistants, such as Apple's Newton, Sony's Magic Link, Motorola's Envoy and AT&T's Personal Link. These wireless handheld devices allow users to transmit and receive information while away from the office. And there are the customized news delivery services from firms like Individual Inc. and Desktop Data, where business people can receive their own "personalized newspaper" delivered every morning to their PC, containing news just on topics previously specified to be of most importance and interest.

Further down the road even more sophisticated personal technology filters are under development. Northern Research, a division of Northern Talcum, has been experimenting with a PDA device called Orbitor that allows users to set their own "personal availability modes." This would allow, for example, the user to instruct their device to allow e-mail or faxes only from people with certain phone numbers, or—during certain quiet hours— from nobody at all. Researchers at MIT's Media Lab are experimenting with software that incorporates artificial intelligence that understands its users' work habits so well that it can make even more sophisticated choices in determining what type of information to find, when to transmit it, and when to forward the data to somebody else.

Technology, though, will not cure your information overload problem: it may offer you more choices in how and when to send and receive information, it may help you locate more relevant information, or it may assist you in organizing your information. However, it will not "solve" the problem. Science fiction author Tom Maddox notes the paradoxical reason why: 'Any device we invent to filter information causes more information to come into circulation than it can filter'.

So just as the early highways laid down by the government to handle the growing number of automobiles spurred even more traffic, creating new information lanes encourage and allow more information to be passed back and forth.

If true, then, are we all doomed to an ever-mounting, out of control influx of information?

Well, it just may be that the amount of information available to you will, in fact, continue to mount. With the explosion of the Internet, especially the growth of the world wide web, anyone today can become his or her own publisher. That's right, the world wide web allows anyone who has a modem to cheaply and instantly disseminate what they've written, designed and produced to millions of people around the globe. We are just at the very beginning of this revolutionary change that virtually eliminates publishing's traditionally expensive barriers to entry: the printing press and distribution costs. So if you are thinking that it can't get any worse, we're afraid that the information explosion may actually just be getting started!

But there is hope. Later in this book, in Chapter 9: A Prescription for Information Paralysis, we outline three specific strategies you can take today to battle information overload and take control of the beast.

1

The New Key to Success

Why is being well informed important?

If you're like most businesspersons, you probably know your own industry inside and out. But it's less likely that you feel quite as well versed in the use and management of business information. And that is unfortunate, since in the 1990s and beyond it will be the companies that know how to use information that will emerge as winners.

What is "information consciousness," why is it so important, and how do you get it? First let's go over a few definitions. For our purposes, information is "meaningful data." Meaningful data is made up of numbers, statistics, scientific findings, new product sales trends, or any facts or series of facts that tells you something you didn't already know and adds to your understanding of whatever you are interested in finding out about. Pure data, on the other hand, is simply a number of facts without a significant relationship to any other data, e.g., Coca Cola's sales were $4 billion in 1990. But if you had that sales data plotted against other soft drink sales for 1990, then you'd have information. And while data leads to information, information leads to knowledge. And knowledge is the inexhaustible resource of the 1990s and beyond.

Although we've known for a long time that knowledge is the critical resource that distinguishes the most successful firms, the hard evidence to back our feeling up is now mounting. An increasing number of forward looking management experts and businesses are looking intently at how to measure and manage their "knowledge assets."

Books, reports, and case studies have been pouring in, all coming to the same conclusion. A study published in 1995 by Ikujiro Nonaka and Hirotaka Takeuchi (*The Knowledge Creating Company: How Japanese Companies Create the Dynamic of Innovation,* Oxford University Press) found that it is the ability to create new knowledge—not manufacturing ability—that distinguishes the most successful firms. Another book, *Working Wisdom: Timeless Skills and Vanguard Strategies for the Learning Organization* (Jossey Bass) explains and analyzes the importance of identifying and measuring knowledge. Linda Thornburg, the author of an excellent article titled "Accounting for Knowlege" in HR Magazine, (October, 1994 pp 50-56) states that "it is an axiom of business schools that things that are valued should be measured." Peter Drucker has gone so far as to say that "in fact, knowledge is the only meaningful resource today. The traditional factors of production have not disappeared, but they have become secondary." (*Post-Capitalist Society*, HarperCollins, p.42)

The business press is also recognizing that, in the words of Skandia Insurance's Director of Intellectual Capital Leif Edvinsson, "a lot of the value of the corporation is in the minds of employees." The title of a *Fortune* magazine cover story in October, 1994, was: "Measuring Your Most Valuable Asset: Intellectual Capital." And *Computerworld*, a few month's later, in an article called "Smarten Up!" instructed its readers that "companies must gather, cultivate and manage intellectual capital as carefully as they do financial capital."

And firms are beginning to do just that. Corporations that have taken steps in this direction include General Motors, Fidelity Inc, Monsanto, Dow Chemical, Hewlett-Packard, AT&T, IBM, and more. Some, such as Ernst & Young, Hoffman-LaRoche,

Xerox and Gemini Consulting have even created a new position: The CKO or Chief Knowledge Officer to coordinate the entire firm's efforts in measuring and managing its intellectual capital.

A slew of more technical and scholarly articles in publications like the *Harvard Business Review* and the *Sloan Management Review* offer detailed methodologies on how to go about measuring intellectual capital and worker knowledge. Of particular interest and attention here are ways to identify what's being called "tacit" knowledge: not just knowing data, facts, and figures, but an employee's ingrained, almost intuitive "soft" knowledge that one gets from being deeply immersed in a field and from years of experience.

All right, you may say, you've made your point: everyone and his brother is saying how important knowledge and information is to business. But come on, isn't that kind of obvious: I mean hasn't learning and knowledge always been important? What's the big deal now?

That's right—knowledge has always been vital for business, and it is a little disingenuous to all of a sudden "discover" its importance. But we think it's like the reasons behind the "total quality" movement: in the mid 1980s, everybody was suddenly interested in "quality." But when U.S. executives went to Japan—the nation that supposedly put TQM into practice—they discovered that Japanese businesspersons thought the whole topic of "total quality" was silly. Why? Because insuring quality was automatically built in to the Japanese's entire design and manufacturing process, and to try to isolate it as some separate entity seemed, to them, absurd. To the Japanese, it would be akin to getting excited about, say, a new manufacturing movement to ensure that all automobiles coming off the assembly line will be drivable.

The Japanese understood the basic truth that quality is not some "extra" separate process to be added on, but an inherent mindset. However, most U.S. business executives did not "get it": and hence, the need for a total quality movement. It was almost like a necessary remedial course to catch up.

And that is where, we think, we are with this nascent movement towards isolating and identifying knowledge assets. It needs to happen in order to put the necessary energy towards understanding and working to ensure that businesses are valuing knowledge in their workers, and putting it to its most effective use.

Now although we've said that knowledge has always been important for business— and this is true—it is also true that knowledge is more important than ever in business now. Here's why.

Since the early 1980s, the business world and its external environment have gone through enormous changes: the pace of business has accelerated from fast to faster to blazing; demographics and consumer preferences are changing; the global market has become a cold, hard reality; the Internet is effecting everyone and everything, and the world is simply more complex.

What this all means is that today, for a successful firm to keep up—i.e. meet changing consumer demands and preferences, and stay ahead of its competitors—it must cut its time to market, reduce R&D time, and overall boost its productivity. It must be fast and it must be nimble. Tom Peters has put it like this: "it's not that small is beautiful—it's just that inflexible is ugly and getting uglier all the time."

How, then, does a company get to be fast and nimble? What does it need to do? Well, several things can do the trick. One is to flatten the organization and cut layers of staff. This reduces the time it takes for information to move and for decisions to be made. And, corporations have been laying off staff since the mid 1980s, and it's still uncertain when this trend is going to slow. Another way to be fast and nimble is to empower front line workers: let them make more decisions on their own, and use teams to help ensure that employees buy in to decisions made and work to implement them, not hinder them. And finally, companies increase their speed and flexibility by utilizing technology. This means installing internal networks so that workers can communicate with each other quickly and share information.

Now, you can see that the single resource that all the above techniques focus on is information and knowledge: moving information quickly up and down the hierarchy, giving line workers the authority to use their own knowledge (the "soft, tacit" kind) to make a decision, and using networked systems to move information up, down, and around the organization as quickly as possible. Everything centers on moving information quickly, so that data can be turned into information and information can be transformed into knowledge. In this way, the firm can move quickly and effectively, and therefore, succeed in the fast moving global market.

It's also important to note that "information" as used here goes far beyond the more narrow definition, where discussion of information systems and information workers referred just to MIS departments or computer hardware and software. A leader in the field of knowledge management, Tom Davenport of Ernst & Young's Center for Business Innovation (Boston) has said that computers and the data in computers cannot solve problems alone; instead one must engage in what he calls "human-centered" information management, which focuses on all sorts of information (not just information stored in computers), and that what's going to count the most and make a difference is examining how people in an organization share and use the information that they have or acquire.

This movement towards identifying and utilizing knowledge has one sacred rule: information, to be transformed into knowledge and to effectively be put to use by an organization, must be shared. Firms are experimenting with a variety of both technological solutions (e.g. Groupware systems like Lotus-Notes) as well as managerial and organizational approaches to facilitate as much information sharing as possible.

The point of this mini-digression into the emerging science of knowledge theory has simply been this: to show that in today's dizzying global information economy, being information savvy is not just useful, it is critical. Alvin Toffler, in his book *Power Shift*, states that today knowledge *is* business, and that what is going to "count most" is knowledge about knowledge. And that's what this book is all about.

2
Never Assume Anything

If information consists of related facts, news, statistics, impressions, and so forth—pieces of intelligence that singly or jointly increase your awareness and build toward knowledge—then what is an assumption? It is a conclusion based upon none of those things. It is a guess, pure and simple—sometimes luckily true, but most often false. While in some cases it may be based on a knowledgeable intuition or a subtle understanding, most of the time it is based on nothing at all.

A book publisher we know decided a while back to publish an anthology of in-depth articles concerning a profession with which he was very familiar. He reckoned that he needed only 30 meaningful pieces to make a fine book. Since there were probably 150 such articles published in any given year, it would, he assumed, be simple to acquire them, winnow the best, and write for permission to reprint. At a high monthly fee he retained a clipping service to find them. Three months and several hundred dollars later, he was dismayed to find nothing. He had made the *assumption* that such articles existed, because he thought that they should. Had he gone to a firm specializing in finding information, he would have learned this in ten minutes at a small fraction of the cost (more about this later). But to have done the latter, it would have been necessary to sidestep his ego and ask a question rather than assume a fact.

People may choose to make assumptions for a variety of ill-founded reasons. Sometimes people make an assumption because they think they *should* know something. Another reason people may make an assumption is that they believe that they are the only one who has ever had this problem (or question), so they have no choice but to make an assumption. But in reality, it's more than likely that many others have had the same problem, and probably have even come up with the answers! Another reason people make assumptions is simply that they just don't know about the plethora of information resources that are available for the asking, and they feel that there's no choice but to rely on guesswork. Again, a bad methodology for coming up with a conclusion.

Don't feel too bad if you have made assumptions in your life. As any librarian or information specialist can tell you, most people are constantly making incorrect assumptions about the types and amounts of information available on a particular subject. One person may expect to find, say, statistics on a small town's soft-drink buying habits, but is then surprised to find out just how difficult such data can be to obtain; conversely, someone else may wonder how there could be anything "out there" on Japanese imports of compact disk players—and that data would be easy to find!

In order to make a good decision, that decision must be based on solid and reliable information. As the saying goes, you've got to do your homework! The alternative—decisions based on no information or on faulty assumptions—can lead to disaster.

To use an example from personal life, how many times have friends of yours complained that they went off on vacation only to be faced with transportation problems, overbooked hotels, wasted time, bad weather, or poor food and service? This type of thing rarely happens to people who are information conscious. When they decide to go somewhere, they do their homework. They have maps, they know weather statistics, they are armed with hotel and restaurant ratings, they've studied articles on the resort. They enjoy their vacation.

Why Do We Assume?

Why do many business executives make assumptions without finding and using information? There are a few main reasons.

First of all, there is no specific and solid education offered on the subject of information. For some reason, most business schools, while offering traditional courses on marketing and market research, haven't really kept up with the changing role of information and its uses outside of the traditional market research function. About the only type of professional that really gets a grounding in the information age and in strategic information-finding is someone getting his or her masters in library science. The problem with most library science courses, however, is that they are usually narrowly structured to match the traditional library needs. But the business world has changed—and is changing—so quickly that a business's information needs are much more complex and strategic than what the traditional library school program provides.

Another reason why most executives are poor information finders is that most have had little actual hands-on experience in finding information. Most of us have some fuzzy memories of a grammar school introduction to the library: we were told how to use the card catalog, where to find the encyclopedias, and why we should keep our voices down. A fine introduction to the information age! And, unfortunately, that's about as far as most of us ever got; in fact, many a self-assured and successful businessperson is reduced to near helplessness when back in a library trying to find a piece of information. Often, after half-heartedly browsing through the card catalog and aimlessly wandering around the bookshelves, the businessperson "assumes" that there's no information on the subject, and walks out of the library disappointed

Don't assume.

Ask Questions

What then is the key to getting information? Information is obtained by asking questions. *Lots* of questions. You start off with a "problem" of some kind, which could be anything: you could be the head of a company seeking to select a new plant site, a marketing executive looking for international sales opportunities, a health food store owner opening a new branch, or a consultant seeking new clients. All problems are different, but the process for uncovering information is the same:

• State the problem.
• Define what information you need.
• Determine why you need it.
• Decide what you will do with it.

One of the secrets to the proper understanding of information is the realization that the information you seek is almost certainly available. Not always, by any means. But the vast majority of the time, some information is indeed "out there" on the topic. The reason for this is fairly simple. You may think that your problem is unique, but it's actually much more likely that others have had the same questions and have done some leg work to dig up answers. The hard part of collecting and analyzing the data is likely already done—now all you have to do is find it!

Herein lies the most fundamental concept in information consciousness. At the risk of boring you, we'll repeat it: rather than making any assumptions that might lead to failure, make the assumption that the information needed for success is out there somewhere and available at a reasonable price. Then go look for it.

A few words of caution: Although it is very likely that the information you seek is already out there, there will be certain cases when it won't be. This is most likely to happen if your question is extremely narrow and specialized. So, for example, if you need to find out how many children under the age of eighteen live in Dallas, you are more likely to find that data than if you wanted to also know how many of those children prefer sugar to cake ice cream cones. The former is data that is collected by the government for statistical purposes; the latter is information you'd likely have to go out and collect yourself by creating a survey or hiring someone to do a survey for you.

Primary Versus Secondary Information

There is a very important distinction between primary and secondary information. Technically speaking, all information can be categorized as either primary or secondary. Primary information is derived directly from the original source providing the data. For example, a "focus group" interview, answers to a political survey, and observations from someone examining traffic patterns are all types of primary research. This is loosely equivalent to what you might call "firsthand" information. A secondary information source is one that takes that primary research and compiles it—often along with other information—in another source, often editing or recombining it with other data. So, for example, a textbook describing political surveys would be a secondary source. Books and magazine articles are also secondary sources.

There are other key distinctions between the two types of information. Secondary information is generally easy to find and is relatively inexpensive. Usually, it's just a matter of finding the right book, magazine article, government report, or published market study. However, if you find that there is no secondary information available, you may have to conduct your own primary research, which can be very expensive.

For example, say you were trying to get a feel for the market for laser printers. You would probably find a lot of secondary information on that topic, such as magazine articles, government statistical reports, and even "off-the-shelf" market research reports. These published reports are typically extensive studies of a defined market, providing key analysis and statistics on items like overall sales, leading companies, foreign competition, import/export figures, trends, technological impact, forecasts, and more. While these studies are not exactly cheap (ranging in cost from about $300 to over $3,000), they are a bargain compared to what you'd have to pay to get an equivalent custom primary study done to meet your needs. Primary research studies can cost anywhere from $10,000 to $50,000 or more. Note that although secondary market studies are normally more than adequate, there are cases when your data requirements are so very specialized or unique in some way that you would want to spring for a primary study.

Internal Versus External Information

Another key distinction between types of information is the difference between internal and external information. In a business context, internal information involves facts about your own company—your sales figures, the number of clients you have, where your products are shipped, etc. Internal information is used mostly—though not exclusively—for the purpose of measuring performance. External information, on the other hand, is information about the world outside your company. It involves facts about competitors, markets, demographics, environment, etc. External information is used mostly for planning and decision-making, although it is obvious that an effective decision to move into a new market, for example, should be based on a careful assessment of internal information (what markets we are in now) and external information (where are the opportunities). This sounds obvious, but apparently is not obvious to the vast majority of executives who make key decisions every day either without much external information at all, or without bothering to combine external information with internal.

Internal information is usually readily available to most of us, because its collection is vital and necessary for a business to operate. When Xerox and IBM talk about information, they are usually actually referring to internal information, because that's the kind of information their equipment is most useful in managing. It's also the kind of information most businesses *must* have.

External information is not usually perceived as being as important. It is more difficult to obtain, and is often neglected—with occasionally disastrous consequences.

The business press is replete with stories of companies and products that failed because changes in the marketplace or demographics—external information—were ignored or never perceived.

Those who inaccurately assume that their assumptions are correct may accurately assume that they, too, will fall by the wayside.

3

Translating Your Problems Into Questions

When the great Gertrude Stein was on her deathbed, a friend came to visit and found Ms. Stein in her final throes. Somewhat delirious, Ms. Stein kept repeating, "What is the answer? What is the answer?" Hoping to hear a final philosophic pronunciamento, her friend leaned forward expectantly. Gertrude Stein's final words were, "But then what is the question?" Probably just a story, but it attests to the heightened information consciousness of that wonderful lady of letters.

What is your question? Oftentimes the question you ask is either obtuse or not the question you really mean to ask. And it's too often the case that you don't ask a question at all. But asking good questions is the key to getting the information you need.

Think about it. When you want a date, you need to ask if he or she is willing. If you feel you deserve a raise, you have to ask for it. And it's no less true that to get answers to your business problems, you have to ask. You *have* to ask questions. Contrary to what some may assume, answers don't magically appear out of the blue. Answers are the result of questions. And good answers are the result of asking good questions. Questions are keys, keys that unlock information vaults filled with answers.

But while it sounds simple, asking questions is not always

easy. In fact, many of us have unfortunately been trained to avoid asking questions out of the fear that we will sound "stupid" or ask a "dumb question." In school, it seemed like the "nerd" was the one who always had his or her hand up asking all those annoying questions. Well, how much would you like to wager that today most of those nerds have carved out prominent and successful positions in their fields?

Even as adults, many of us shy away from asking questions. Some people will drive around, lost for hours, determined to "find it" themselves, instead of taking thirty seconds to ask a question and get on to the destination.

But it's the person who isn't afraid of asking a question, isn't afraid of how the question sounds, and isn't afraid of the tiny risk in requesting an answer who comes out on top. The old cliché that "there is no such thing as a stupid question" is very true: asking a question—any question—is simply a method or technique to get what you need. In this case, what you need is information, and you get information by asking questions. It's the key to improving your information consciousness.

If you don't have questions about your profession or your business or the ways in which you are conducting them, you should question that! It means you have a very low level of information consciousness. And you are not alone. When asked what is the single biggest sales resistance they encounter, the salespeople of a leading information and research service firm reported very simply that business executives say they have no questions!

Once you've convinced yourself that asking questions—lots of questions—is not only acceptable, but absolutely vital for getting what you want, you then need to know a little bit about the art of asking a "good" question. This doesn't mean that asking a "bad" question is stupid. It just means that some types of questions are going to be more fruitful in eliciting the most useful types of responses. But any question—no matter how "bad"—is better than not asking any question at all.

How do you go about coming up with good questions that will yield the answers you seek? The key is to know the procedures to follow. It's a thinking process and, like most techniques, there is a bit of an art to it.

Business Problems Are Information Problems

Interestingly, most executives will readily admit that they have plenty of problems. So the first step is to think of problems (and opportunities) as information needs, as series of questions that need to be answered. *Every problem that relates to a business or profession ultimately boils down to an information problem.* We think we have *decision* problems. But if we had a sufficient amount of information, all correct decisions would be indicated in that information. That's why it's so important, when thinking about problems, to think information. That's information consciousness.

All businesses have problems of one sort or another, even if they are not urgent ones. For example, here are some typical problems a business marketing a new baby food might have:

- Determining what type of customer to target.
- Deciding whether to sell the product overseas.
- Figuring out how to sell to customers in another country.
- Choosing between competing computer-system networks.
- Selecting a new product or service to introduce.
- Deciding how to price the product.

Now, if you say that you just don't *have* any problems, something isn't right! It means that you do not see any opportunities, areas for growth, or new horizons. And if that's the case, you really do have a problem—a big one—since it means you aren't moving forward. As Woody Allen told Diane Keaton in *Annie Hall*, "A relationship is like a shark—if it doesn't keep moving forward, it dies." The same is true for a business. Don't end up a dead shark.

Another reason for a low level of information consciousness is the lack of discipline in a logical progression of thought. Let's assume that you want to eat at a very fine French restaurant next Saturday evening. Lack of this discipline of logic would find you downtown that evening without a reservation, poking your head into a number of restaurants, checking prices and menus, being turned away by some, etc. In short, it would be a hassle.

The information-conscious reaction to this problem would be: My problem is to find a good French restaurant. So I need information about restaurants. Someone has probably had the same problem before. There is probably a guidebook on restaurants in this area. It may indicate which are French, plus facts on quality, prices, hours, atmosphere, and so forth. So if I find the guidebook, I solve my problem. Obviously, this is a simplified example. But the principle can be applied universally.

A young lady we know had a very typical problem. She needed to find a job. She had spent three years in a liberal arts college, then spent ten years in Italy married to an actor. While in Italy she became fluent in Italian and did some odd jobs translating, dubbing films, and so on. She later got divorced and returned to New York, desperately needing a job. She had no college degree, no office skills, and no real full-time job experience. For days she floundered around, visiting friends of friends who supposedly would help her and contacting employment agency after agency where all she was asked was how many words per minute she could type. Finally, she consulted our information-finding firm. We applied some information discipline to the problem. The lady's assets included intelligence, language, affinity for the film business and other creative arts, and knowledge of Italy. The information steps required were:

• Get a list of all Italian companies with offices in New York. Contact them, giving priority to those involved in the arts.

• Visit the commercial attaché of the Italian consulate to find out what companies might be expanding or opening offices in New York.

• Find out which employment agencies specialize in bilingual jobs and which specialize in the music and film industry. Contact them.

• Get a list of companies in New York in the film, recording, artistic management, music, and television industries. Contact them.

• Get a list of all leading translation firms. Contact them.

The young lady found an excellent position.

In a business setting, the first step in following the discipline of logical progression of thought is to come up with a list of all your business "problems." The next step is to translate those problems into questions. This isn't really a very difficult task, and just requires you to "see" your problems in a different light and rephrase them.

So, for example, say that you were considering exporting that new type of baby food. Your business problems might be these:

• You need to know what type of persons would most want to buy your product.

• You need to know what regions of the world would be most receptive.

• You need to know why people in those regions would want to buy your product.

• You need to know what kind of computer system to get to organize your operations.

• You need to know why those buyers would choose your baby food over competitors' products.

• You need to know how much to charge for your product.

We could then translate these problems into preliminary questions:

• What are the demographics and purchasing habits of people who buy baby food?

- What countries have a need and a demand for this type of baby food?
- What are the demographics and cultural considerations of persons in those countries?
- What are my needs in a computer network? What do I want to be able to achieve?
- What do buyers of baby foods want that they currently aren't getting?
- What do competitors charge for a similar product? What will most people pay?

Here's another example. Say your problem was whether or not to sell frozen bagels in Europe. You could break this larger problem down into smaller, more answerable questions, and then subdivide those questions where possible. Here is a very simplified illustration.

Problem: *Should we sell frozen bagels in Europe?*

Now break this problem down into smaller questions.

Which countries are most likely to buy frozen bagels?

a. What are the demographics of people who buy this product?
b. Where can I find an analysis of demographics of various European countries?
c. Which countries' populations match up with those characteristics?

Say you've chosen France as a potential market.

What are the legal and regulatory requirements for importing food products in France?

a. Which United States government offices provide data and advice on selling overseas?
b. Which offices in France can tell me of their governmental requirements?

What is the competition like for frozen bagels in France?

a. What are the names of companies already selling this product?
b. Where can I find a market study analyzing sales and market shares for frozen bagels in France?

Breaking Problems Down

As you can see, the art of creating good questions means going through the process of breaking up a large, seemingly unmanageable problem into smaller pieces. Here are some other tips to help you ask for information in a way that will produce the best results.

❏ DETERMINE WHY YOU NEED THE INFORMATION

The reason behind any request is usually obvious. Yet a very clear and precise understanding of why information is needed is often lacking. For example, if you need a specific fact—like the 1988 sales of Perrier—to toss into a speech, you should ask for exactly that. Asking for a "run-down" on Perrier will increase the cost of the research, and may not even yield the sales figure you need. On the other hand, if you need background information to assess the market potential for a new kind of bottled water, then asking for a profile of the bottled water industry may be an excellent broad question. In any case, tell whoever is going to look for the answer why you need it. An understanding of the reason is vital to a successful search.

❏ TRANSLATE YOUR INFORMATION NEED INTO A QUESTION

Even when you've clearly established why you need information, formulating a good question can be a challenge. For example, say your company's sales compensation plan needs revamping. You want information to help you do it. You could ask for any available data on sales compensation plans. But such a request may produce huge masses of mostly useless information. Try asking instead, "Are there comparative studies of sales compensation plans that will tell me the norms for my industry?" This type of precise question could produce an equally precise answer.

❏ MAKE YOUR QUESTION SPECIFIC

Your real question could be a general one: "Will a branch office I am contemplating in Des Moines succeed?" Unfortunately, no one can answer this question as stated. But consider asking specific questions like: "What is the population of Des Moines?" "What is the political climate in that city?" "Who are my competitors there?" Combined answers to these questions, properly interpreted, will help you make an intelligent and successful decision.

❏ ASSESS THE VALUE OF YOUR QUESTION

Having a sense of the value of the information you need can help you phrase your question. Do you need the information for a low-priority idea you're working on? Did the boss ask for it? Is it related to a new $10 million product development plan? If you have some idea of the value of the information, you'll be better able to phrase your question and give critical guidance to a researcher. (You wouldn't want your secretary to spend a full day trying to find a hotel room in New York if there's only a 10 percent chance you'll go there.) More on the value of information in Chapter 4.

❏ DESCRIBE WHAT YOU ALREADY KNOW
ABOUT THE ANSWER

You may already have part of your answer. For example, you want to know total United States distilled spirits sales in dollars, but you already have the figure in units. Or maybe there are some sources you've checked before without success. By all means, let your researcher know about the background information you have and where you've already looked. Much time is lost when people neglect to do this.

❏ DETERMINE THE AVAILABILITY OF THE INFORMATION YOU NEED

If you're not a researcher, you won't know what data is available and what is not. But a little careful thought on your part can tell you how likely it is that an answer will be found. For example, common sense should suggest that finding an already published marketshare breakdown of baby carriage sales for three counties in Idaho would be virtually impossible. Asking for a list of all the major department and discount stores in the top cities in Idaho is a question that probably can be answered, but common sense should suggest that it may not be answered in five minutes.

❏ DO THE ASKING YOURSELF

Remember the telephone game? Ten people line up, and the first says a brief sentence to the second, who repeats it to the third, and so on. By the time the tenth person has heard the sentence, it has completely changed from what the first person said. If you have a question and want to get an answer, don't relay your request through a third party, like your secretary. Telling someone else to ask a question for you will almost insure that the answer you get will not be the one you needed. Always ask your own questions.

❏ DO YOU NEED AN ANSWER OR JUST A SOURCE?

This is an important distinction many people fail to make, especially when they are using someone else to perform their research. Generally, the more specific your question, the more you need an actual answer. If your question is very broad, you may wish to browse through the source yourself. In the example cited above, you might well need the answer to a specific question on population in Des Moines. But if a good fact book existed on the Des Moines area, you would want to examine that as well.

Typical Business Questions

Many people in business have told us that even when they are in a frame of mind to ask questions, they're not exactly sure what to ask questions about. They often feel that their particular problem or question doesn't relate to any information that may be available.

While we can't tell you what your own questions should be, we can dispel once and for all the notion that information may not be available. *You can and should ask questions about anything.* In most cases, information *is* available.

To suggest the endless possibilities, here's a sampling of how executives in various functions are getting results through asking questions:

• When the president of a major pharmaceutical company felt that he might have to justify his research-and-development expenditures at the next stockholder meeting, he asked for and got data on the research-and-development expenditures of ten similar firms.

• When back-up data was needed for the development of an electronics company's five-year plan, the planning director obtained information on typical industry financial ratios, articles on current management practices in the electronics business, data on exports, and a study of the industry's future in Europe.

• When the chairman of a major chemical company decided to look into potential acquisitions in the solar energy field, he began by obtaining an overview report on the industry that identified three potential targets, two of which were later researched in depth.

• The marketing director of a company with a new bottled water subsidiary wanted to expand to Florida. He asked for a list of competitors in that state and then commissioned an in-depth study of the industry in Florida, including interviews with companies in the field.

• A sales manager scheduled an important meeting with a key prospect. Doing his "homework" beforehand, he dug for and unearthed vital facts on the prospective client, biographical details on the principals involved, and several published articles on the company and its industry.

• A disposable diaper firm became concerned about long-range sales forecasts. It collected birth-rate projection statistics through the year 2010 and used them to develop year-by-year data on the size of its potential market.

• A printing products manufacturer wanted to introduce a new line. He obtained an overview of the market, had an outside company research the alternative methods of distribution to end-users, and commissioned a survey of distributors. He was then able to competently determine his product introduction strategy.

• A public relations manager who needed to develop a campaign concerning diabetes figured that celebrities could help. He asked for and got a list of famous people who have the disease.

• A company president's son was seriously ill with a form of colitis. Instead of merely consulting the leading local specialist, the president first obtained a list of virtually every article published on the disease in medical journals over the past ten years. He then obtained copies of the articles, read them, and through them identified the four or five leading specialists on the disease in the world. He also obtained background on the major drugs used to treat the disease. Then he took his son to the best doctors, armed with sufficient knowledge to discuss the case intelligently.

And here is just a brief sampling of requests recently handled for business executives by a qualified information-finding firm, along with the reason behind each request:

• What was last year's consumption of imported beer in the United States? How much was imported from each country? (To establish a company's import guidelines.)

• What is the profitability of the health club business? (For an executive considering purchasing a franchise.)

• Are there any businesses with United States offices that specialize in the rental of ski chalets and apartments in Europe? (To find a way to plan a three-week stay at a ski resort in Switzerland.)

• What is the cat population of the United States? How many live in metropolitan areas? (To help plan distribution for a pet supply firm.)

• What were the top two songs of 1952? (For planning an anniversary celebration.)

• Please provide all demographic information on chain saw users—who uses them, where, and how often? (For a firm that produces a safety accessory.)

• The Indonesian government has new export regulations. What are they? (To help in the negotiation of an importing contract.)

• How do you spell the actual sound an owl makes? (For copywriting an advertisement.)

• Please obtain results of studies on the toxicity of benzoyl peroxide. (For assistance in complying with environmental regulations.)

• Please obtain a list of New York's richest men. (We thought this might have been for an ambitious single lady, but actually it was to help write a magazine article on expensive cars.)

• Who designed the L'Eggs Panty Hose display rack? (For someone who needed a package design and liked this one.)

- Do food additives have any known adverse effects on child development? (For the public relations manager of a food additive company.)

- I need background on the industries and resources of one of the new republics that was formerly part of the Soviet Union. (For an executive who was scheduled to meet with the premier of the republic.)

Other questions that businesses frequently ask include:

- Where can I find demographic information on potential clients?

- How do my competitors distribute their product?

- Where can I find a suitable partner overseas for a joint venture?

- Is now a good time to get into this market?

- Are my customers satisfied with my product?

- What is the background of the new executive my competitor has appointed?

- What are the sales and revenues of the top companies in this industry?

Any questions?

4

The Price and Value
of Information

What is information worth? How much should you be prepared to pay to get the facts you need? While most of us are conditioned to see the cost of something only in monetary terms, in the business and professional sphere it is necessary to equate cost with *value*. And the value of information is assessed by examining the time and money spent in acquiring it.

Time is precious. It is also finite. No matter how we try, we cannot increase it. No matter how much money we spend, we cannot gain more time.

Three factors must be considered when assessing the cost of information: time, money, and ultimate gain.

Information Is Never Really Free

Most of us think that public libraries and the information you find there are free. This is not really accurate. While it is true that the facts and data themselves may be "free" in that the resources are there for anyone to use, the finding, collecting, and locating of information takes time; and time, as the saying goes, is money. Even for the most mundane tasks, there is a time cost in uncovering information. For example, if you need to fly to Seattle, and you or an aide spend two hours finding out all the flight and accommodation details, you will have used up valuable time; if instead you called a travel agency, the fee for that call would be the only cost factor involved.

What about the Internet? Isn't there a lot of free information available? Again, it depends on how you define the question. Yes, a good deal of information available over the Internet is available at no charge; however, you must still pay an Internet service provider or consumer online service like America Online to get access to the Internet. Also, to a large degree, what you find on the Internet reflects the old "you get what you pay for" axiom. A lot of the free information on the Internet isn't worth your time in finding it and reading it.

And that, again, is the real point, and the real cost in finding information. Even more so than on traditional databases, you can easily get sucked into spending hours and hours on the Internet, hunting for information, getting lured into an interesting site, just to realize that it's a dead end, or losing your way among a series of hyperlinks. Even Alvin Toffler, one of the original gurus of living in the information age has reportedly said that he doesn't even use the Internet because it takes too much time!

It is incredible when you realize the number of important, high-salaried people involved daily in the drudgery of finding information of one type or another. It's incredible because, first, the information has been gathered before and, second, it's available at a price. If you have raised your level of information consciousness sufficiently to be aware of these two things, then you are already halfway toward answering your question. Therefore, you have saved 45 percent of your time (money). This is true because, when there is an information problem, 90 percent of the work is in finding the sources, and 10 percent of the work is in using the source material to get the answer.

Having said all this, though, we must acknowledge that the Internet has, indeed, had a tremendous impact on how information is viewed, and in accelerating the concept of information as a free resource. Although, as stated above, we take exception to that notion, there's also no question that the Internet does represent a new paradigm for information dissemination. The usenet discussion groups, for example, represent the availability of nearly free information: they are resources of experts and expertise easily available to anyone, anytime.

What this means is that if you can learn how to effectively use newsgroups to get fast answers to your quick questions, you will have tapped into a source of virtually free information (we say virtually free because there is still normally an Internet access fee, and there is still a time cost to joining and querying a news group). The savvy businessperson then, will use the usenet groups and selected portions of the Internet as a very fast and cost-effective tool for quickly finding experts and expert opinion at nearly no cost. See Chapter 8 for more information on using the Internet for business research.

Here is another notion that blocks information consciousness. Many people believe that they must always do their own research to benefit from the information gained. This is normally *not* true, and can be very inefficient. Trying to find information on your own can be costly. In addition to the cost of your time, you must also add what is called the "opportunity cost." Let us assume that you hire someone whom you pay $20 an hour to do work for which you bill your clients $100 an hour. If that person does research for your own company's use, you would assume that this costs you $20 an hour. Right? Wrong! It costs you $120 an hour, because you are also losing the one hour of income that person would be producing. And it will probably take this person twice as long to get the information as it might take an information expert.

This is not to say that there is no point to performing some research on your own. In certain circumstances, for example when launching a new business or entering a new market, it is very important for the businessperson to do at least a little research in order to experience firsthand some intangibles, such as the "flavor" of the market being researched. This could be a matter of making just a half dozen phone calls to supplement the full research effort.

So information is *not* free, as there are various cost elements involved in locating and finding it. But how much is the information actually worth? Ultimately, a piece of information's value depends on how much it aids you in making the best possible business decision. What's it worth to you to be able to make better decisions? You can't put an exact figure on it. But it's clear that better decision-making is what everything in business ultimately boils down to, and any resource that will improve decision-making is an extraordinarily precious one. Information is such a resource.

What's It Worth to You?

Things get tricky when we try to determine precisely how much a particular piece of information is worth, and to assign to it a specific dollar figure. Information's value is subjective. A piece of information may be worth exactly $1,000 to you, may be totally worthless to me, and may be worth $10,000 to the next person. Here are some illustrations of this point:

• The A.C. Nielsen Company does a continuous study that includes a measurement of the movement of different brands of corn flakes through supermarket outlets on a week-to-week and year-to-year comparative basis. This service sells for thousands of dollars per year. This study, needless to say, would be worthless to the owner of a "mom and pop" grocery store. It would be worth its price to a marketing consultant to the corn products industry. But it might be worth at least ten times its price to the Kellogg Company.

• The results of a survey done in October 1991 on the growth of the bottled water industry are available, let us say, for $300. The data is accurate and was compiled by a reputable firm. But there is a problem. The bottled water industry has been growing by leaps and bounds since 1991, and much has changed radically. If there has been no similar study since, your only alternative would be to conduct your own up-to-date survey at a cost of

$20,000. What is the value of the $300 report? It would depend on (a) whether you have just a passing interest in bottled water, (b) whether you intend to open a million-dollar bottled water plant, or (c) whether you are an advertising agency on the verge of making your pitch to a potential account that bottles water. The $300 report is worthless to (a) because information must be acted upon to have value. It is also worthless to (b) because the information is too old to base a million-dollar expenditure on. It may have some value to (c) as background material to impress the prospective client.

• Let's border on the science-fictional and assume that it would cost $2 million to determine the number of bricks in all the buildings in Manhattan. Would anyone spend that kind of money for such seemingly worthless information? Maybe—the used brick dealer who was just authoritatively and secretly informed by a seismologist that Manhattan will be totally destroyed by an earthquake within twelve months.

• Back to more mundane matters: The price of *The Guide to Restaurants* is $10. Would it pay to research the credentials of the author and the publisher? Not if you only intend to use it once for locating a restaurant. But yes it would, if you are a publisher contemplating issuing a competing book on that subject.

• It can cost $100,000 per year or more to set up, staff, and maintain an in-house library. Is it worth it? You can answer the question yourself now by simply asking this question: Worth it to whom?

So, like beauty, the value of information is in the "eye of the beholder." But assigning a particular value to information is even trickier when you consider that not only is information's value totally subjective, but it also depends, to a great extent, on the potential costs of *not* having that information. For example, not too long ago, a gentleman approached a research firm requesting patent search and engineering information on a new textile manufacturing process. As a result of the data, he was able to sell his product to Hanes Panty Hose for approximately

$10 million. Without that information, as he later told the information service that uncovered the data, it would have been nearly impossible to have landed that contract. So, assuming that without the data he could not have made the deal, that information was worth $10 million! You need to try to figure out what the potential costs of not having the needed information could be. While in some cases it may not be much, in other cases you could easily be talking about thousands or millions of dollars.

Perhaps in part because the cost of information is difficult to define, the value of information is very subjective, and information itself is an intangible, many people confuse the value relationships involved. Either they believe they can get lots of information for a little money, or only a little information for a lot of money. They ask a question that they believe will cost little to answer, because the answer is of low value to them. Or they ask a question that they believe will cost a lot to answer, because the answer is of high value to them. In fact, as often as not, the low-value answer may cost a hundred times more than the high-value answer.

The Hard Costs of Information

How does the information-conscious person deal with this problem? First, you should never make a firm assumption about how much you *think* it will cost to obtain whatever information you seek. Second, always be prepared to accept that the information you want may not be available to you at a price you are able or willing to pay. Third—and most importantly—understand that virtually any question can be answered for $50, $500, $5,000, $50,000, or more. It all depends on how much time is spent looking, and on how much depth and detail is required. This is one of the most important concepts in the information field, because it can help you scale the level and cost of the research to the value of the answer to you.

Let's apply this concept to a specific problem and see what

levels of information can be obtained, and for what situation each level is most appropriate.

Assume you are interested in a particular industry or market. It doesn't matter whether it's licorice, light bulbs, or lipstick. Here's a rough idea of the information you might get at the various cost levels:

• *"Free" (a call to the library)*. Not truly free—your taxes have paid for the library, and you must use your time to place a call or make a visit. The librarian might be able to look up a trade association's address and phone number for you, or read a statistic out of a popular handbook like the *United States Industrial Outlook*. This approach is obviously suitable only when you just need a readily available single fact, or if you are prepared to spend a lot of time in the library.

• *$10–$250*. For this amount of money, you could do your own online search or hire a research firm for an hour's work and obtain a few statistics on the market, find a few trade magazine articles, or get names of leading companies in the field. This approach is useful when you need quick general information or a brief consultation.

• *$500–$2,500*. In this cost range, you should be able to get a more comprehensive overview of the industry, based on a gathering of readily available secondary data. A reasonably comprehensive—but not exhaustive—search of published literature would be included. Major articles from trade journals, basic government statistics—essentially anything that has been collected and published. All of this could be useful for background information, speech making, report writing, and early stages of planning and problem solving.

• *$5,000–$15,000*. Based on the secondary information gathered above, plus more exhaustive searching and limited telephone contacts with trade sources, a 20- to 100-page profile of the industry could be prepared in this cost range. The profile would cover the size of the market, companies in the field, distribution patterns, regulations, etc., though not with the depth and detail of the next level up. It would also be useful for the initial stages of studying an opportunity, a new product, a new venture, or an acquisition.

• *$10,000 and up.* At this level, a full-scale industry and market study can be produced. It would include a fully exhaustive search of secondary data; extensive interviews with trade sources, manufacturers, retailers, and other industry components; careful study of market potential and other factors affecting the industry—all embodied in a report, with summary and analyses, that might run up to several hundred pages. In these higher price ranges, a customized survey of consumers (whether individuals or other businesses) would be included. This type of in-depth study is essential for all advanced stages of planning, product introductions, acquisitions, and so forth.

Types of Information-Providers

Another way to perceive the cost-value problem is to look at the broad categories under which information can be obtained from the vast array of publishers and information-finding organizations. Although it may be difficult for you to determine exactly how much a particular piece of information is worth, those who sell information must indeed do just that and come up with a hard price. Different types of information-providers have created different methods for pricing their information services. The following types are listed in order of least to most costly.

❏ ONLINE DATABASE PROVIDERS

Producers of online databases charge an hourly rate, based on the amount of time the user spends electronically connected to their system. Rates vary quite a bit, but typically run about $60–$150 per hour of online search time, with an additional cost added for each item retrieved (this may range from 10¢ to $10 or more per item). But in this case, remember, it is your time that you are spending doing the search, and there is no human "expertise" being bought—just the ability to quickly access and search already collected data. For more details on locating information from online databases, see Chapter 7, which is devoted to this subject.

❑ PUBLISHED STUDIES

Sometimes information has already been gathered and put into printed form, with a set price established by the publisher. The publisher generally tries to establish a competitive price based on what others are charging for similar reports, and on what the market will bear. There is a wide price range for published market studies and reports. Typically they cost anywhere from $200 to $500 for the smaller ones and from the low to mid thousands for large and detailed studies.

❑ MULTICLIENT STUDIES

A special category of published reports is "multiclient studies and surveys," which are "sponsored" in advance, usually by a limited number of organizations. The sponsors can then request additional, highly specific questions they want answered as part of the study. This makes multiclient studies more useful to them than ordinary published studies. In the case of consumer surveys, multiclient studies are often referred to as "syndicated research."

❑ INDIVIDUALLY CONTRACTED STUDIES

These are ordered and paid for by a single entity, to whom the results belong exclusively. "Custom" studies and surveys of this kind may, of course, fall within a very broad price range, depending on the information needed, but typically are the most expensive type of information that can be obtained, as they often involve extensive primary research.

The special types of firms that carry out these contracted searches for information are called information-finding or research services. Many of the smaller ones call themselves "information brokers"—independent firms that perform research for a fee. Reva Basch, president of the Association of Independent Information Professionals, explains that information brokers sell their expertise in knowing how to locate information, and not the end result. In fact, when you engage the services of such a firm, you do not know what the results will ultimately be. Occasionally, an information search may even turn up "nothing" at all. But the fact that there is nothing on a topic could be of great value in certain instances (e.g., an inventor who wants to find out if there are already any published references to his new product idea). So when you hire someone to locate information for you, you generally do not pay for the actual data uncovered, but for the time and expertise required to find it. Information-finding firms and brokers typically charge an hourly rate ($50–over $150) plus any direct costs incurred.

The foregoing example should suggest points that cannot be repeated too often:

• Information that has already been published somewhere is much less expensive than information that must be gathered and developed on a customized basis.

• "Raw" information (a bunch of statistics from a book or copies of articles) is much less expensive to provide than any kind of written summary or report based on that information.

• In the case of large studies and surveys, it is always cheaper to purchase "off the shelf" than to contract for customized research.

• The more important the use to which the information will be put, the more exhaustive a research job should be done.

• Collecting secondary (published) information is much less costly than conducting primary original research.

Failure Costs

At this point you may say to yourself, "You've told me that information is not free, and you've told me something about its cost and value. But how do I know when it's really worth spending money for?"

The answer is that you may never know, because the true value of information is often measured only in relation to the cost of the failure that results from not having it.

We once knew two salespersons who worked for the same company. They sold the same line of products to the same types of customers in similar territories. They both had the same background and experience.

Yet John, the first salesperson, earned close to $80,000 a year, while Harry, the second, only managed to earn $40,000 a year. Harry was a good dresser, a smooth talker, and a hard worker who wined and dined his customers regularly. He was, in fact, a good salesperson. In an attempt to find out why John was twice as successful as Harry, the sales manager visited John at his home. There, in his basement office, was a veritable Library of Congress. There were complete files on each of John's customers. For each company, he kept computer records on its history, earnings, and plans. He had tear sheets of its advertisements and online printouts about its marketing practices. He had information on each of his customer's problems. There was even a complete rundown on the executives he contacted within those companies—their hobbies, family, club memberships, and the like. In short, John had a lot of information; Harry had very little. The information was worth $40,000 to John; the lack of it cost Harry at least $40,000.

A good way to measure the value of information comes from an older, but still valid and enlightening, article in the May 15, 1976, issue of *Boardroom Reports*, (now called Bottom Line Business) which makes a comparison of "failure costs." According to that study, the likelihood of the failure of a $100,000 project is one in three without research, so the failure cost is $33,000. With research, the risk of failure is one in five, for a failure cost of $20,000. The value of the research is then the difference between the two costs, or $13,000.

In summary, information is not free. It takes time and resources to gather it. The value of a piece of information depends on the circumstances, and on the potential costs of not having that information. There are different ways of obtaining information, and the cost of each level of information service varies. The key is to match your need with the appropriate level.

5

How to Judge
the Quality of the
Information You Get

Back in the early 1980s, if you picked up any of a handful of market research studies on the emerging home "videotext" industry, you would have read that the industry was poised to explode during the decade and experience tremendous growth. And, after reading such reports, you might have decided to enter that market, or invest in a company in that field. However, the only thing that home videotext experienced during the 1980s was a spectacular *lack* of growth. And any business that decided to enter that market based on those forecasts most likely ended up losing money.

So far this book has examined the importance of having information consciousness and of asking good questions. But another vital issue is determining information reliability and believability. Although we are, indeed, in an "information age," and surrounded by data and facts of all kinds, separating the good information from the bad is not necessarily an easy task.

You can see that this is true not only in the business world, but in day-to-day personal life as well; for example, in the new forms of "news" called infotainment and docudramas, it's nearly impossible to determine where the facts end and the fiction picks up. And it seems almost impossible to decide which of the latest scientific studies to believe. Does eating oat bran lower cholesterol? Is drinking two cups of coffee a day okay? Clearly, more information doesn't always mean clearer information, or ultimately make it easier to make decisions.

In the business arena, scores of competing data sources are created and churned out by a wide variety of firms. The developers of these information sources, like other vendors, make claims of having the best, most complete, or most useful "product." But completeness and quality vary between sources, and the well-known warning of *caveat emptor* applies to buyers of information, just as much as it does to buyers of other goods. Information has become another *commodity*, and you, the customer, must be alert to its quality and reliability.

And now, we have the Internet. That wonderful, amazing, omnipresent source of virtually all human knowledge, now accessible to all of us at the push of a button. Unfortunately, too many official sounding information sites and sources on the Internet are simply the work of, say, a college sophomore whose main critiques of another's view is to repeat "that really sucks." Not exactly the same level of discourse that you might find in a peer-reviewed AMA journal.

This is not to say that the Internet is not of value for the business researchers. In fact, it can be of enormous value, as explained in detail in Chapter 8. But if its been a case of "buyer beware" for users of traditional sources of business information, it's now got to be buyer (or net-surfer) be afraid...be very afraid.

The problem isn't that there isn't good "stuff" out there on the net—there's a lot: government economic reports, public company filings, stock quotes, newswires, scientific lab reports, and so forth—it's just that so much of the time you don't know who is behind the information you've uncovered, and what that person or institution's credibility is. At least when you buy a report from, say Dun & Bradstreet or download an article from *The Economist* from the ABI/Inform database on Dialog, you know, based on past experience and those of colleagues, what you're likely to get. But on the Internet, although, like Alice's restaurant, you can "get whatever you want," too often, you don't know who the chefs are or whether they have even cooked before.

Another problem with information on the Internet, is that the data itself is becoming increasingly decontextualized. Because of the capabilities of hypertext technology, users can now locate articles without getting the entire publication; pages of articles minus the complete article; sections of pages without the full page; and bits of data by themselves. So although there are countless additional pure facts and pieces of data "out there," the surrounding context that puts it all into some perspective is often missing. This, then, leaves it up to you to figure out the context. But if you fail to do so, you only get data, and not information or knowledge. And it's information and knowledge that makes all the difference in business—not just the facts alone.

So, the problem of knowing who to trust and who to believe, when it comes to evaluating information has gotten much worse, rather than better, since this book was last updated "all the way back" in 1993—before the emergence of Internet for the masses.

In addition to distinguishing good data from bad, today's smart information users need to have the ability to properly interpret and analyze data. Misreading what data is telling you can be just as dangerous as having no information at all. Just remember what happened to American car manufacturers in the early 1980s when they misjudged consumer demand for smaller and more fuel-efficient cars!

No Source Is Perfect

What are some of the most common quality and reliability problems in business information sources? You might be surprised to discover that even supposedly "unimpeachable" sources can contain errors, be misleading, or be misinterpreted. Take, for example, the "bible" for United States statistics, the *Statistical Abstract of the United States*. Some years ago the volume contained several critical number transpositions. And if you don't read the fine print on how to use the data—and honestly, how many of us really do?—it's very easy to misunderstand such vital things as units of measurement, years covered, and other key supporting data that you must understand in order to know what you're really reading!

So the first thing you should be aware of is that no source is perfect, and that you should never assume that the data you have obtained is necessarily correct. The simplest and best method for checking reliability is to consult a second or even a third source. Now, of course, if there are no other sources, you will have to rely on the particular source you are using—however, there are still other methods you can use to help ascertain the reliability of a unique source, as described at the very end of this chapter.

Although it is true that you should never assume any single source is perfect, it is also true that some types of sources are more likely to have reliability problems than others, and that some data quality issues are of highest importance. A description of some of these "high profile" information quality areas follows.

❏ COMPANY DIRECTORY DATA

One of the data sources most commonly used by businesses are company directories. Company directories list key facts on businesses, such as their address, total sales, names and titles of key officers, products and services produced, and so on. Some directories have even more information, such as market share, profit and loss statements, subsidiary linkages, and so on. These are vital research tools that are used regularly by almost all business researchers. Some of the most well-known directories include *Dun & Bradstreet Million Dollar Directory*, *Standard & Poor's Register of Corporations, Directors, and Executives*, and *Ward's Business Directory*. These can normally be found in print form, as well as online.

Unfortunately, while these are immensely valuable guides, they can be filled with inaccuracies. Typos, outdated information, and poor data collection methodologies all are causes of frequent errors.

There are a number of reasons why. One, according to sources within the industry, is that for a variety of motivations, ranging from tax purposes to establishing of credit, an owner of a business will sometimes overstate or understate sales figures. Unlike the Securities and Exchange Commission, a directory publisher has no legal recourse should a firm provide false data. Probably even a more common source of bad data is the directory publisher's failure to update old information. Smaller, private, and lesser-known firms receive less attention from directory providers, and there are likely fewer checks on data accuracy—though big mistakes can occur with larger firms, too. A while ago, we performed a computer search to locate presidents of major companies, and found that the computer database listed a secretary at Canon as the firm's president; and for Eastman Kodak the database listed one of the company's marketing directors as the president! The sad thing is that such incidents are not all that unusual.

❏ MARKET SIZE AND FORECAST REPORTS

Like company directories, market size and forecast reports are frequently used by business, but are also frequently wrong! These reports, which are issued by various well-known—and not so well-known—research firms, all purport to measure the size of a particular industry or product, and frequently forecast growth into the future as well. So, for example, such studies might tell you things like how many home healthcare diagnostic kits were sold last year, or the expected number of CD-ROMs to be sold through the year 2000, and so on.

However, measuring the market size of an industry or product is a tricky business—and forecasts are even trickier! Let's look at a study that attempts to measure the number of laser printers sold last year. The key question, of course, is where is the publisher going to find this information, and how is he going to make a count? There are a variety of methodologies that can be used, some more reliable than others. Most rely on a sample survey of some kind, and these may be conducted in a variety of ways. Some try to talk to buyers and measure placements by analyzing the demand side, but a more reliable method is to survey manufacturers and measure the supply side. There are other ways in which survey methodologies differ, e.g., whether the survey is conducted by mail or by phone, and whether the sample is truly representative of the population being measured. Other important issues relate to what type of person answers the survey, and whether that person truly has the knowledge and ability to provide accurate answers.

In addition to these difficult statistical and methodological problems, you need to be careful for fast moving industries, that the market research report is still timely. Business conditions change so quickly these days, that sometimes the useful shelf life of a market research report is extremely short.

As uncertain as market size measurements are, forecasts are even more so. When it comes right down to it, you have to remember that a forecast is really nothing more than a guess. Now some guesses are going to be more educated than others, and some will be based on better information than others, but predicting the future is not exactly one of the hard sciences. Just ask any meteorologist!

The best forecasters have a track record in successfully measuring the specific items being studied and a complete understanding of the product, industry, or whatever else is being measured. A good forecaster tries, as much as possible, to take into account any upcoming technological, sociological, and demographic trends that could impact growth. And, importantly, a good forecast provides not just figures and tables, but lots of explanatory text that describes the underlying assumptions and methodologies, and shows the user how best to use the information presented.

❏ POLLS AND SURVEYS

Polls and surveys are notoriously unreliable. Conducting a proper poll or survey of people's opinions or habits is a true science that demands a high degree of knowledge about technical issues like random sampling error, non-sampling errors, non-response errors, and more. Some popular surveys, such as magazine reader surveys, are conducted in flagrant violation of these rules, and their results, consequently, can be virtually worthless as any true measurement of people's opinions or behaviors. Other polls may make some effort to avoid the most obvious accuracy problems, but still end up with such a large margin of error that relying on their results is, at best, extremely risky.

In addition to poor data collection and measurement methods, polls and surveys can suffer from a variety of other problems:

• Organizations with a specific agenda can word questions to elicit desired responses or interpret results in a manner to serve their aims.

• Placement of questions can impact respondents' answers.

• Choice of words and "loaded" phrases can influence respondents' answers.

• People often knowingly or unknowingly give wrong answers, due either to faulty memory or a reluctance to provide honest answers. People are particularly prone to providing incorrect answers to sensitive questions, or ones that they perceive as reflecting badly on them.

The best advice we can provide on using polls and surveys is to always confirm any results by checking other sources, and not to rely on them alone in making any major business decisions.

Other Information Quality Problems

The following are other factors that can trip up business information users.

❏ BIASED INFORMATION

When reading any report, study, or article, always find out who sponsored the report, why it was issued, and what the aims of that sponsoring organization are. Whose "ox will be gored" by the publication of such data?

❏ NEWSPAPERS

Daily newspapers operate under the heat of a deadline, and errors can and do occur. Newspapers have a tendency to "over interpret," and of course occasionally to sensationalize findings of a single study or incident. For example, a recent Boston study that found that oat bran did not lower cholesterol was played up as the new definitive conclusion on the matter when, in fact, it was only one of a number of serious studies whose findings were still being debated.

The New York Times is considered an authoritative newspaper. But say, for example, that it publishes a figure for United States sales of soft drinks in an article about CocaCola. That figure may come to be taken as gospel and be reprinted in other publications, even though the reporter writing the article may have obtained the figure from the National Soft Drink Association, which may well have conducted a poor study. Many associations publish figures about the size of their industry, and these are sometimes the only figures available. Yet those figures often come from a poll of the association's members, which may have been conducted unscientifically, or may suffer from the fact that the respondents may not have the incentive to answer with complete candor.

❏ OUTDATED INFORMATION

Is the information provided by the source up-to-date? Is it first- or secondhand? How did this source actually come up with this information? These are all key issues that reflect on the reliability of the source. To take a very simple example, the recognized authoritative source for demographic information is the United States Bureau of the Census. The data is firsthand information, obtained through exhaustive survey procedures (complaints about certain under counts notwithstanding). Yet, the last complete census prior to publication of this book was completed in 1990, so the data, while from an authoritative source, is a few years old by mid-decade. Unfortunately, aside from periodic, limited updates and projections, there are no real alternatives.

❑ ONLINE INFORMATION

It might seem to some people that information found online via computers is more trustworthy than other information. This is nonsense. Data found via computer is at least as likely to contain errors as information found in print. For more information on computer databases, see Chapter 7.

❑ MASSAGED INFORMATION

Finally, the manner in which information is presented can significantly affect your use of it. Most information that has been assembled from statistics, data, facts, etc., has been "massaged" in some way before it gets to you. Massaging is the putting together of data in a manner that applies to a particular problem at hand. For example, let us assume that information concerning birth statistics in Indiana is required. Many different types of such statistics may be available from several different federal, state, and local agencies. Gathering all of these statistics together, it may become necessary to create charts or graphs (or both) to make the data intelligible. If ten people created charts from the same set of statistics, we would have ten different charts. This is because each person would "massage" the information in a different way. All the different charts may be correct, yet the way the information is presented will affect how the data is interpreted.

Say, for example, you wanted to know total dollar sales of widgets in the United States in 1994 and 1995. You might be shown a simple table like this:

1994	1995
$175,000,000	$182,000,000

Or, using the same data, you might be presented with a table like this:

(Millions of dollars)		
1994	1995	% Increase
$175.0	$182.0	3.8%

The second table is not only easier to read, but it presents more information using the exact same data. Reading the first table, you might quickly grasp that widget sales were up by $7 million, but you might miss the fact that the increase was only 3.8 percent—*less* than the inflation rate for that year.

Proper and accurate interpretation also depends upon your own abilities of perception. Always bear your original question in mind and pay close attention to such things as scales and legends on graphs and charts.

To continue our example, assume you commission a study of the widget industry. The researcher you assign to the project returns with a graphic representation of the trend in widget sales at the National Widget Company. (See Figure 5.1.) Initially, you're not likely to pay too much attention to the scale on the graph. You'll look at it and see widget sales trending down slightly. A different researcher doing the same graph could use exactly the same data and present it on a graph with a different scale. (See Figure 5.2.) Now you take a quick look at the graph and exclaim, "Widget sales are crashing!" The difference in your perception is caused by the scale of the graph. Obviously, data can be manipulated to suit anybody's purpose.

Always use your intelligence and common sense. Assume you wanted information on the microprocessor industry. You can't afford to commission a study, so you ask if one has already been done and is available in published form. Say you find a study, and it's "only" one year old. But if you know anything

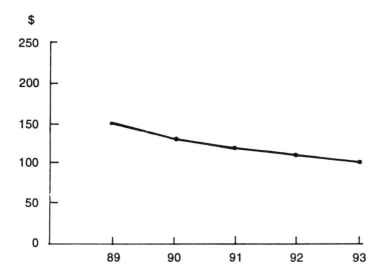

Figure 5.1   The National Widget Company's sale of widgets depicted on a graph using a scale of $0–$250 million.

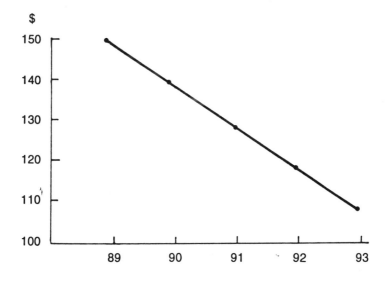

Figure 5.2   The National Widget Company's sale of widgets depicted on a graph using a scale of $100–$150 million.

about the industry, you'll know that in a year's time, the industry and products change drastically, and so the study would only be of limited value.

The main point to keep in mind is to always be skeptical when using information. Here is some basic advice to better insure that the information you use is accurate and trustworthy:

• Know your subject. The more you know about the topic you're researching, the less likely it is that you'll be misled by bad data.

• Identify the best "brand names" in your information sources. Determine which databases, journals, or even individual writers are on target most often and the most insightful. Then, look for, track, and obtain as much as you can from those sources. One of the biggest problems of the Internet age is knowing who to believe: by proactively determining ahead of time which ones are most useful and reliable for you, you can cut through some of the information fog.

• Talk to people. When you find pieces of data in print or online, treat them as leads, not as final answers. Run the data by some knowledgeable persons and get feedback.

• Use more than one source, if possible, to compare data.

• If you have questions about data, call the provider and ask him or her to identify the original source of the data. Ask about data collection techniques. Are you satisfied with the answers you got?

• Track down authors of articles and market studies, and interview them. You'll get clarifications and analyses not provided in the published piece, and will get your own questions answered.

• Don't pay too much attention to forecasts. Remember what they are—guesses!

• Always check footnotes, units of measurement, explanatory material, etc. Sometimes, the smaller the print, the more significant it is.

• When reading a study or analysis, find out the purpose of the publication or sponsoring organization. Is it purely to collect and publish data, or are there any political, ideological, or other agendas?

• If your goal is to insure as high a degree of accuracy as possible, use primary over secondary sources.

• Try, as much as possible, to obtain skills, knowledge, and training in the field you are researching

• Cultivate the art of critical thinking. Don't accept what you read as gospel. Get confirming sources, ask questions, talk to experts, probe for motivations, and use your intuition—if something just doesn't sound right, check it out further.

Finally, remember that unused information is useless. An encyclopedia is worthless if never referred to—as is any dictionary. So many professionals and business people subscribe to much-needed trade literature and even commission studies without ever glancing at them! Then there are those who read the information, but never use it. To be of value, information must be acted upon. If it is ignored, it is valueless. Too busy? If your competitors find time to take advantage of the world of information, you will soon find yourself with nothing to be busy about.

6

Welcome to the Age of Information

Okay everybody, put down what you're doing! Look ahead, take note, stand up, pay attention! The "information age" has arrived! From this day forward, your lives will forever be changed!

Such is the sense of drama that usually accompanies a description of the new information environment. But what does that catchy "information age" phrase really mean? Few of us actually stop to think about what an information age is and what it means to live during such a time. First, let's recognize that the information age has come about even faster than you might imagine: the widow of Marconi just died in 1994!
Information has become the major force propelling society. It is the fuel that turns the wheels of modern business and modern living, and makes them "run." Let's look a little closer at how this all came about.

Information itself, of course, is hardly anything new. The storing and sharing of knowledge has been going on since before humans started writing on stone and papyrus. A giant leap forward occurred when the printing press was invented, as it allowed facts to be easily communicated to anyone at virtually any place. From that time, up until about the middle of this century, people found information either by going to a library or by purchasing encyclopedias and other reference books. Later, they were able to utilize special information services, such as Dun & Bradstreet's credit reporting services, which actually started before 1900.

The Computer

Then, in the middle of the twentieth century, a number of developments occurred that helped create today's new information environment, or information "age."

The most significant of these developments was the invention of the computer. The computer brought tremendous advances: it massively increased the amount of information that could be collected and stored; provided the power to combine, edit, and synthesize collected data; and made it simple to provide instantaneous transmittal of data to anyone anywhere who had access to a computer terminal. And all this power was accomplished by standalone computers. By the late 1980s, the real power of the computer was harnessed by linking them into networks. This occurred first over internal networks, then via wider networks linking organizations across larger physical boundaries, and finally over the Internet, which, can link together anyone around the globe with access to a pc, a modem, and a reliable phone line.

At the same time, society's need for information accelerated rapidly. The world became more complex: disciplines grew increasingly narrow and specialized; heavy industry gave way to services and knowledge-based businesses; communications and transportation advancements brought together people and their ideas from around the world; and an international emphasis on technology spurred a faster race for scientific and technical data. Each of these phenomena fed off the other, creating a spiraling demand for more information on more topics—to be delivered much faster.

In response to this ever-growing demand for facts and data, traditional book and magazine publishers geared up and began producing more information, and in additional formats (e.g., microfilm, computer tape). At the same time, firms other than traditional book and journal publishers entered the business of producing information; many of these specialized in providing data via computer tape, or remotely, "online."

The United States government, as it expanded its roles and services during the 1950s, 1960s, and 1970s, became an enormous producer of all kinds of information, ranging from highly technical and scientific reports and journals to consumer advisories to business development guides—and countless other documents. Companies and organizations set up in-house information services departments and computer networks in order to collect, manage, and disseminate all this external—as well as their own internal—information, so as to make better decisions.

The Information Industry

All of this information activity gave rise to a new "information industry," which is composed of a variety of subdisciplines and segments. To get an idea of the types of businesses that are an integral part of the information industry today, consider the following list, which names just some of the leading organizations in the field:

- *Association of Independent Information Professionals.* This is an organization of independent firms that sell information-finding services. These information-finding firms are also known as "information brokers."

- *Association of Information Managers.* This association consists of information managers and executives in corporations and government dedicated to advancing the information management profession.

- *American Society for Information Science* This is an organization composed of individuals interested in the science and theory of information technology and related topics such as storage and retrieval of data.

• *Information Industry Association.* Members of this organization include the very largest of the information companies, e.g., AT&T, Dun & Bradstreet, Knight Ridder, McGraw-Hill, etc., and are concerned with "macro" issues affecting their industry, such as governmental regulations, competition, new technology, and so forth.

• *Society of Competitive Intelligence Professionals.* Individuals who belong to this group perform "competitive intelligence" for their companies, and their duties include finding data on competitive conditions, monitoring competitor activities, and so forth.

• *Special Libraries Association.* This organization is composed of librarians who do not work in a "traditional" library setting. Many corporate librarians and "information specialists" belong to this group.

The Information-finding Field

Who are the people that belong to these groups? What sorts of jobs are directly linked to the information industry? Since virtually everyone's job involves finding, managing, and disseminating information, it's no exaggeration to say that everyone is involved in some way in the information industry. But there are certain jobs that are directly and exclusively devoted to the information field.

Probably the most visible of these jobs is the librarian, or more specifically in business, the company or corporate librarian. Although company librarians have been around for a long time, because of the enormous changes in the use and management of business data, during the last ten years or so corporate librarians' jobs and duties have changed. In fact, many of them no longer even call themselves librarians, but instead prefer other titles like "information manager" or "information specialist." Such titles better reflect the varying and more sophisticated roles of today's corporate librarian, who almost always performs such tasks as computerized database searching and, in some organizations, strategic monitoring and collection of information on specified industries and companies, as well.

The most forward-thinking business librarians have also taken on the role of becoming their firm's information and knowledge resource coordinator. They do more than conduct research and search databases: they look at how their firm is using information on an organization-wide basis and initiate and engage in projects that improve the entire firm's strategic leverage of information. These jobs include things like mapping how information flows within the company, conducting information audits, partnering with the IS department to deliver just-in-time news and documents over internal networks, evaluating electronic desktop news delivery services, and training staff on use of the Internet.

A number of individuals who have had traditional library education and experience have left their field (sometimes of their own initiative, but often as a result of staff cutbacks) and set up their own information brokerage (also called information-finding) firms, through which they sell their expertise at finding information and searching online databases. Many businesses that do not have complete expertise in finding information or performing searches hire information brokers to do the job for them.

While many of these information brokerage firms are small, sometimes consisting of a single individual, there are a few notably larger ones. Our firm, FIND/SVP, Inc. of New York City, is perhaps the largest and most well-known of these. Established in 1969, FIND/SVP is now a publicly-held company (NASDAQ-FSVP) with revenues of nearly $30 million and a staff of 275. It provides quick consulting, research and advisory services by telephone, and currently answers over 8,000 questions a month for 16,000 executives in more than 2,200 firms that are retainer clients. In addition, FIND/SVP offers a variety of other custom research, competitive intelligence and consulting services and products.

Many companies have created new staff positions just to take advantage of the new information environment. For example, most Fortune 500 firms today have employees whose duties relate specifically to finding information on competitors and competitive conditions. This new field has given itself the name "competitive intelligence" to describe its function. Typically, persons involved in this field perform strategic monitoring of key data sources such as online databases, government filings, Securities and Exchange Commission reports, and other sources of facts and insights on the competition. Depending on the particular "culture" of the firm, a competitive intelligence function could be located within the library, strategic planning, marketing, or market research departments.

Another position is the CIO, or Chief Information Officer, who is the person in charge of a company's entire computerized information resources. These resources usually include management information systems and electronic networks. The newest information related position, is Chief Knowledge Officer or CKO. This person directs and coordinates his or her company's strategic use of all information—not just those held in computers, but those in people's rolodex, file drawers—and most importantly—information that's ingrained and expressed by workers as skills, entrepreneurial capabilities, and tacit knowledge.

Other jobs directly involved with information are those held by market researchers. These people are typically responsible for a wide variety of data-finding and analysis operations, including both quantitative and qualitative surveys.

Finally, there are the producers and resellers of all this sought-after information. These include traditional book and magazine publishers, organizations and institutions that gather and sell facts and information of special interest, database creators that put all that information into electronic searchable formats, and online "hosts" that resell and distribute the database producers' products. For more information on the online database industry, see Chapter 7.

A Sampling of Resources

The new information environment has emerged so quickly that few have learned how to use it. Yet it has changed the way sophisticated companies and executives do business. Here are a few examples of what this new information environment means to businesses:

• If you want to know about something, the fact that it can probably be found is not so farfetched when you realize that a summary of virtually every major article in the business press published in the past five years is stored on computer and readily retrievable in the space of a few minutes.

• If you sell to consumers, there is a wealth of consumer purchasing-power statistics readily available, including a myriad of breakdowns by zip code.

• Are you looking for new suppliers overseas or keeping tabs on competitive importers? There's a computerized service that keeps track of imports into the United States for various commodities by country and port of origin, port of arrival, and consignee!

• Want to pinpoint your marketing? Simply select the industry you market to, the size of the company that makes the best customer, the title of your typical buyer, and the zip codes where you'd like to sell. A printout of prospective customers' names can be on your desk within minutes.

• Need to find a manufacturer or retailer in a certain region of the country? Today the entire country's yellow pages can be searched on a single computer CD-ROM disc.

• Want key facts on a company you're researching? All public companies must file extensive financial reports with the Securities and Exchange Commission in Washington, DC. Most of those statements and supporting documents can be accessed in seconds.

• Want to sell your product in other countries? The United States government has set up an entire department within the Department of Commerce devoted to providing free and cheap information to businesses that want to sell their products or services overseas.

• Looking for the right consumer? The Bureau of the Census sells a geographical mapping system called "TIGER" that can pinpoint by zip code the exact demographic characteristics of the neighborhoods you want to reach.

• Want to check out whether a patent has been filed on a new product? Patent and trademark searches can be done from the comfort of your computer terminal.

• If you need to track news developments around the world, you can choose from a handful of international news wires that are updated every fifteen minutes.

• Need to see how your investments are performing today? Financial markets and stocks can be tracked minute by minute in "real time."

• Worried about competitors in Europe or Japan? If you need to check facts on foreign competitors, full-blown statistical and analytical reports are ready for your review.

• Are you wondering what people are thinking and saying about a new product, your company, your competitors, or another topic? You can "listen in" to electronic conversations over the Internet's newsgroups, where people from around the globe discuss and debate everything from aardvark raising to zipper technology.

The above list doesn't even begin to scratch the surface of the types and amounts of information available today for the asking. In fact, for many people, all of these wonderful data resources have caused the "information overload" problem we discussed in the introduction of this book.

It is true that there is now such an enormous amount of facts, data, statistics, reports, and studies being produced and disseminated that businesses can easily feel overwhelmed and even paralyzed. For some, there's so much "out there" that the job of deciding which source to utilize becomes a confusing and overwhelming task. That's why it is so vital that businespeople become information-conscious, learn about the information environment around them, and discover how to search for answers. Such knowledge, while not eliminating the possibility of having an "information anxiety" spell, will provide you with the confidence and skills you need to best understand and utilize information.

Future Resources

If we peer just a bit into the future, we can get a glimpse of some fascinating developments expected to occur in the information industry. For example:

• The hottest and most exciting new information technology are what are called "intelligent agents." This is a type of software that understands the information needs and habits of the user, and can therefore search for relevant information, automatically route it to the user just when he or she needs it, sends the information to other people the user would want to also see it and screen out unwanted information. Some basic and early versions of intelligent agents are already offered by traditional online vendors such as Individual Inc. and Dow Jones Inc. but the more sophisticated versions are still under development. (The cutting edge research is being conducted at the Massachusetts Institute of Technology Media Lab in Cambridge).

• Instead of the slow, manual key-in process that many database producers use to convert "hard copy" data to online form, the increasing sophistication and reliability of scanners and bar code readers will speed the process and help further digitize tons of data now in hard copy form. Everything from the White House budget to the papers in your file drawers are candidates for a quick conversion to digital format.

• As the business and information world becomes even more international, additional data from non-United States sources will become more available. This will expand the "information explosion" even further and will present increased opportunities for those who know how to selectively use this information.

• Automated language translation devices are another upcoming development. Sometime in the not-too-distant future you may, for example, be able to access a Japanese document directly online from Japan, and then have your computer instantly translate the report into English.

• Another example of information manipulation is "custom publishing." In 1990, the publisher McGraw-Hill, in a joint venture with R.R. Donnelley printers and Eastman Kodak Company, developed a system that could produce "customized textbooks." Educators can select specific sections of a textbook based on their particular needs, and combine it with their notes and other items to create their own customized book. This electronic system can even repaginate and create a customized table of contents.

• One stop document delivery firms. There are several information companies, such as UMI and Uncover who have been working to create one stop search and document delivery services. These systems allow users, in one fell swoop, to search multiple databases, view documents in their full, original image format (not just straight ascii text, as had been the traditional format), and then, with a push of a button, instantly order that article or report, and have it sent via e-mail, fax, or overnight.

• The Virtual Library. A hot topic in the library field is the emergence of the "virtual library." The concept is that because of technology, libraries may no longer need to be a physical "place" with hard copy books, magazines, and journals to be kept on the shelves, just in case a patron needs them. Instead, a virtual library can be run by just a single person who has electronic access to documents and materials in digital form, and only when a patron makes a specific request, will the "cybrarian" search for and obtain the document over an electronic network. Then, the document can be delivered to the user in electronic form over an internal network or a larger one like the Internet. The virtual library is more likely to emerge in a business environment than a public or academic one, and, while many business information centers are moving in this direction, it is still not completely practical because so much of the world's information is still found only in print and has not been digitized.

• Everybody's a publisher. The world wide web on the Internet has made it possible, for the first time in history, for anyone with access to a PC and a modem to be a mass publisher. Traditionally, the barriers to publishing were the expenses associated with the means of production (printing presses) and distribution (delivery trucks, getting shelf space, etc.). However, the Internet truly allows anyone with a little creativity and a bit of technical know-how to create their own "home page" on some topic, and then make it instantly available to over 30 million people around the globe.

• A global consciousness. Even more futuristic and provoking then the aspect of everyone becoming a publisher, are the predictions as to what will happen when the minds of millions of people connected over the Internet can be put together, thereby bypassing the limitations of both physical space, time, and economics in bringing people together. While the implications of this are far broader than what's covered in this book, the outgrowth of such a phenomena is sure to impact the information age, and how we all create, view, use, and share information.

These developments are happening fast: in fact, in our last edition of this book, published in early 1993, one of the future predictions was the increasing emergence of "hypertext" systems: software that organizes and links different kinds of information together in a non-linear manner. Well, the Internet's world wide web operates by using such hypertext technology, and is the fastest growing portion of the net. So hypertext is no longer something coming—it's here!

Data Privacy

One issue of continuing sensitivity is "data privacy." Credit bureaus, marketing companies, and other firms that make their living by collecting and selling data about people are finding that the public is becoming increasingly disturbed by unwanted intrusions into their private matters. For example, after privacy objections were voiced, a major information-provider, Lotus Corporation, recalled a planned CD-ROM product that would have listed demographic data on 80 million households. State governments have filed suit against the largest credit firms for allegedly keeping old and inaccurate data in their files. And Congress has been considering a variety of bills that would provide the public with greater protections from external uses of private information.

On a similar note, as more companies set up a competitive intelligence function within their firms, there is increasing attention and awareness of the kinds of information-finding techniques that could be considered unethical, or even illegal. Recent articles in the popular press have described a number of cases where a company's quest for information on its competitors went too far. Such inappropriate information-gathering activities, which are sometimes termed "industrial espionage," run the gamut from outright theft of documents to wiretapping, looking through trash, and telephoning and questioning competitors using an assumed name and phony purpose.

Hewlett-Packard, among other companies, has developed an ethics policy (called the "Standards of Business Conduct") designed to prevent unethical information-gathering activities. Hewlett-Packard's policy on obtaining competitive information reads as follows:

> Hewlett-Packard [HP] is entitled to keep up with competitive developments and may review all pertinent public information concerning competitive products. However, HP may not even attempt through improper means to acquire a competitor's trade secrets or other proprietary or confidential information including information as to facilities, manufacturing capacity, technical developments or customers. Improper means include industrial espionage, inducing a competitor's personnel

to disclose confidential information, or other means that are not open and aboveboard.

Your company may want to consider creating its own ethical guidelines for information-gathering.

7

What Computer Databases Can Do for You

Do you feel a little confused about online databases? That's understandable. In fact, it's understandable if you feel very confused! Even in today's age of the Internet and high technology, the word "database" is still one that you'll hear people use without really knowing what it means.

Believe it or not, databases have been around for hundreds of years. Surprised? If so, it's probably because (like many people) you confuse the concept of a database with online databases. It's only the latter that are high-tech and computerized. Strictly speaking, a database is actually nothing more than a collection of information (a base of data). For example, your Rolodex is a database of the phone numbers of your business contacts. Your phone book is a database of names, addresses, and phone numbers of people who live in your city. Your top file drawer may be a database of correspondence you recently mailed out. So, there's nothing mysterious or futuristic about a database!

But—once you take that ordinary database, put it onto a computer system, and create an "online database," you have indeed taken a giant leap forward. For then you have created a powerful information storage and retrieval system.

Some databases are bibliographic, storing the full text or references to and summaries of articles in periodicals, journals, newspapers, and the like. For example, articles from *The New York Times* are stored on commercially available databases like Lexis-Nexis and Dialog.

Other databases store an incredible amount of statistical data, such as demographic statistics, econometric data, stock and bond prices, buying power information, and the like. For instance, the *United States Prices Data Bank* (available through Data Resources, Inc.) stores consumer, wholesale, and industrial price indices complied by the Bureau of Labor Statistics. The *Value Line Data Base* (maintained by Arnold Bernhard & Co.) stores financial data on United States firms.

Still other databases keep track of things like foundation grants, research in progress, patents and trademarks, available technology, and government documents. For example, a database called *CIS Index* (produced by Congressional Information Services) covers United States Congress publications, hearings, House and Senate reports, etc.

Some databases specialize in forecasting and allow you to perform correlations and analyses. Some databases include complex econometric models that enable users to measure alternatives through mathematical simulations.

There are now thousands of different computer databases in existence, and the number is growing daily. They include literally millions of items of information readily retrievable by anyone with a computer terminal. The databases are created and maintained by a wide variety of organizations, big and small, public and private. These database "producers" include press organizations like Associated Press and Reuters, public institutions like the National Library of Medicine, specialized technical information producers like Predicasts, and so on. Most of them have only become available since the 1980s.

As will be discussed further in this chapter, these databases are made available from a variety of outlets and organizations: directly from the database producer itself, from consumer online services like America Online or Compuserve or professionally-oriented services like Dialog, on a CD-ROM, from a private information-finding firm, or over the Internet. The point is, no matter where you find access, you absolutely must know about database searching. Using online databases for efficient, timely business research is de rigueur in the 1990s.

Why Use Online Databases?

Databases can be searched by the use of virtually any computer terminal connected to a modem. Through your computer terminal, you can "dial up" a database directly, or connect to a "vendor" that provides access to dozens or even hundreds of individual databases.

The process of looking for information in a database is called a "search." To perform a traditional search, you sit at a terminal, dial an online database or vendor, and select the individual database or databases to be searched. To ask the particular database chosen for specific information, you enter an appropriate set of terms, and, in a matter of seconds, the computer responds with an answer that appears on your screen. You are then usually given the option of printing out the information if you so desire. The typical printout will show either the series of statistics requested or information about published articles on the subject, often including brief abstracts or summaries. Note that while some databases are able to provide only one- to two-paragraph summaries or "abstracts" of original articles, many other databases can provide the complete original text, or even images.

The world of commercially available online information systems is just about thirty years old. But it has already dramatically changed the way many leading corporations and sophisticated information users gather data. It has been estimated that in 1965 there were probably fewer than 20 databases commercially available to the public for information retrieval purposes. Today there are more than 8,000.

Why use a computer database? Computer databases provide enormous advantages and benefits in locating information.

❏ MASSIVE SIZE

Online databases are normally kept on huge data storage devices. These can store literally millions of information items, or "records," in online lingo. It would be literally impossible to manually search through this amount of information, but with access to an online database, huge data banks can be scanned in a couple of minutes.

❏ TIMELINESS

When you go to a library to do research, you might consider yourself lucky if the source you find is dated no farther back than a few months. But if you're searching an online database, you're quite likely to utilize information produced sometime this week, yesterday, or even an hour ago. Databases vary in how often they are updated, but some are updated on a daily basis, and a few are updated every fifteen minutes!

❏ EASE OF ACCESS

Remember our discussion of the value of your time? Well, which would you rather do—spend a half day at the library or fifteen minutes on your computer? With a computer, modem, and communications software, you can bring mountains of data to you without going to the mountain yourself. An accomplished librarian's average time for a manual search of the published literature on a subject might be three and a half hours, whereas the same search on a single database can yield better results in five to fifteen minutes. The results will be better because in that space of time the computer can search through millions of items in a consistent manner. (It is important to note that many public libraries—and most college and university libraries—now offer online services.)

❏ KEYWORD SEARCHING

One of the most powerful aspects of online databases is their capacity to be searched via "keywords" in "Boolean logic." What this actually means is this. Say, for example, you need to find out everything you can on the outlook for decaffeinated coffee beans in Switzerland for the year 2000. If you tried to get this information by going to the library, you'd have to first check indices under a single term (e.g., coffee beans) and then wade through piles of articles and reports to try and find any that covered your specific inquiry. But when searching an online database, you can instruct the computer to locate precisely what you need—and only what you need. So, in this example, if you searched an online database of market forecasts, you could instruct the computer to retrieve only those that mention Switzerland, decaffeinated coffee, and the year 2000.

Many of the newer database vendors utilize "relevancy ranking" search engines for making matches rather than the traditional Boolean method. In these cases, the system examines the frequency and placement of your keywords against the items searched, and returns a list with a numerical ranking for each item that indicates how relevant each is to your search.

What Types of Online Databases Are There?

Today there are over 8,000 different databases covering almost as many subjects, ranging from agriculture and architecture to trade names and textile technology. Databases consist of individual items or "records," which consist of different types of information, depending on the nature of the particular database. For example, some database records consist of magazine article abstracts; others list company names and addresses; a different set may include market research studies; and so on. Here's a sampling of what types of databases exist today:

- Abstracts from management publications.
- Aerospace references.
- Banking news.
- The Bible.
- Biotechnology industry news.
- Chemical substance news.
- Company Securities and Exchange Commission filings.
- Computer news.
- Copyrights and trademarks.
- Defense Department contractors.
- Dun & Bradstreet credit reports.
- Environmental data and news.
- European company data.
- Foundation grants.
- Geological information.
- Market research reports.
- Medical news.
- Merger and acquisitions filings.
- New product announcements.
- Pharmaceutical industry news.
- Popular magazine abstracts.
- Psychological studies.
- Public opinion polls.
- Reuters News Service.
- Toxic chemicals and effects.
- Transportation research.
- World patents index.

Now, at this point, you might be saying to yourself, "Okay, data-bases sound great, but what do they mean for me?" What they mean for you can be summarized in three very simple rules of thumb:

1. Frequently, gaining knowledge means finding out quickly what has been written about an industry, a product, a company, a management technique, an individual, a place—anything. Databases can tell you in minutes what's been published about almost anything.

2. At other times, gaining knowledge means that you need some hard statistics. Databases can be used to retrieve an enormous amount of collected information, ranging from census data to patent data to governmental statistics to financial data to facts on foundation grants.

3. Finally, you may wish to have some fact, publication, or quotation at hand. Many recent databases make entire publications such as encyclopedias, newspapers, directories, and even the Bible available for you to "tap into" for a specific fact or paragraph.

We can broadly group databases into four major categories, based on where they are made available. These categories are:

1. Consumer online services.
2. Professional hosts.
3. Business end-user systems.
4. The Internet.

Although there is overlap: e.g.. a database on a consumer online service may also be available from a professional host or on the Internet, etc., there are some significant differences in how these various providers make databases available and how you can search them.

Consumer Online Services

The major consumer online services: America Online, CompuServe, Prodigy—and most recently, the Microsoft Network—all make searchable databases available. However, except for a few notable services on CompuServe, databases on consumer online services are not typically too powerful or very flexible. Often, their coverage is shallow (in terms of amount of time span covered and number of journals or data items included), are not designed for sophisticated keyword searching, and are not as timely as they should be.

The notable exception to this, though, is CompuServe, which makes available two very powerful professional database search services: Knowledge Index, a low cost subset of about 100 databases from the professional Dialog database collection, and IQuest, a much more expensive but powerful link to hundreds of professional online services. Microsoft Network is also introducing a selection of in-depth business information sources; it is the newest of the consumer online services, though, and it is still early to tell how extensive its offerings will become.

Professional Hosts

There are several professionally-oriented providers of the more powerful online databases. The big names are Dialog and Lexis-Nexis; though there are others such as DataStar, which specializes in European information; DataTimes, which offers the full text of many daily newspapers and NewsNet for access to hundreds of professional industry newsletters.

There are some significant differences between databases offered from a professional online service, and those available from a consumer online service. Databases available from professional vendors normally contain a long backfile, include data items from hundreds or even thousands of leading journals, publications, reports, and other top sources, are updated on a timely basis, and can be searched in a variety of powerful and flexible ways. They are also much more expensive: a typical search may easily cost $25-$50 and up.

Business End-User Services

The newest category of database providers gear their offerings specifically for businesspeople who are not librarians or professional researchers, but who want to be able to do their own online searching. (These are called "end-users" in database lingo).

Companies that have introduced search systems for this market include Profound Inc., University Microfilms International's (UMI) (ProQuest Direct), and DataTimes' (EyeQ). Each of these vendors offers windows-compatible graphical interfaces, as well as other innovations that make online database searching easier. They also offer a lower flat-rate pricing plan. As such, these vendors straddle a kind of middle ground between consumer online services like America Online and CompuServe and the traditional professional vendors like Dialog and Lexis-Nexis. Like the consumer online services, they are designed to be simple to use, pleasant to look at, and not too expensive; but like the professional hosts, they also offer extensive business information and high quality business sources. These firms' innovations represent the direction that the online industry is headed towards: even the traditional professional vendors are starting to offer similar features in their services.

The Internet

A full discussion of the Internet is provided in the following chapter. But let's mention here that the kind of information one finds on the Internet is not typically the same as the tightly structured and well-organized information one finds on professional or even on the consumer online services. Mostly, it's bits of unsourced data, snippets of opinion, advice, and conversation. But there are also, hidden among this random "stuff," lists of valuable governmental information, compilations of data from universities and research institutes, and access to at least some traditional databases.

But the real difference in searching for information over the Internet, versus the other providers, is that the Internet is not set up for efficient, linear searching. Instead, it's often a matter of browsing around, checking out sites, and finding something of value. (More on this in the following chapter on the Internet.)

Real Examples

The rules discussed above suggest the versatility of online databases and their usefulness to you. But rules of thumb aren't necessarily as helpful as real examples. How can online databases really help you? What does the information really look like?

Let's now take a handful of typical business problems and see how they can be solved by searching online databases.

For each of the following problems, we searched appropriate online sources to come up with the needed information. The results of our searches, in printout form, are shown below each problem, and appear exactly as they would on your computer if you were searching yourself.

Generally, we have shown only a small portion of the information retrieved, just to give you a quick idea of what you get. Keep in mind that most of the searches were performed in late 1995. You would get much more up-to-date information if you performed the same searches today.

Also note that searches are normally printed out on paper that is eight and a half inches wide. Here, the printouts have been reduced in size to fit this book. In the original, larger size, the material is easier to read, although we point out that lots of type squeezed anywhere is not highly readable. But that's the format most databases use.

Because searching the Internet is so different from searching traditional databases, our examples are drawn only from the latter. Later in this book, under our full discussion of the Internet we will show you what some Internet searches look like.

❏ PROBLEM 1: CALLING VIETNAM

Your company makes telecommunication products, and you want to expand your market. You remember reading that Vietnam, now open to U.S. trade, is exploding as a potential export market. Is this true? Are there really new trade opportunities in Vietnam? You turn to a database on Dialog called *Trade & Industry Index* to find out.

After inputting our search, we can tell Dialog to show us just the headlines and titles of some relevant sounding articles, as a "first cut.":

1. Can a socialist republic find happiness trading in a capitalist world? (China and Vietnam)
WORD COUNT: 2530   LINE COUNT: 00216

2. Sourcing in Vietnam: an EPZ grows in Ho Chi Minh City. (Ho Chi Minh City, Vietnam, Export Processing Zone)
WORD COUNT: 897   LINE COUNT: 00086

3. Vietnam: the current legal environment for U.S. investors. (Silver Anniversary Essays)
WORD C: 3962   LINE COUNT: 00330

4. Vietnam: the satcom protocol. (export laws on satellite communication equipment)(includes related article)
WORD COUNT: 1337   LINE COUNT: 00113

5. Vietnam starts from scratch. (international trade) (Global Report)
WORD COUNT: 583   LINE COUNT: 00046

6. American businesses bank on: global marketing. (opportunities for U.S.corporations in Vietnam)
WORD COUNT: 493   LINE COUNT: 00041

The next step would be to look at the most promising of these in more detail. Items number four and six look intriguing; we can instruct Dialog to provide us with a short abstract of these two:

Vietnam: the satcom protocol. (export laws on satellite communication equipment)(includes related article)
Manuta, Lou
Satellite Communications, v18, n5, p18(2)
May, 1994
ISSN: 0147-7439   LANGUAGE: ENGLISH
RECORD TYPE: FULLTEXT
WORD COUNT: 1337   LINE COUNT: 00113
SPECIAL FEATURES: illustration; graph; photograph
INDUSTRY   CODES/NAMES: TELC   Telecommunications;   AERO
Aerospace and Defense

DESCRIPTORS: Satellite industry—International trade; Export controls—Laws, regulations, etc.; Communications satellites—International trade; Vietnam—Relations with the United States; United States—Relations with Vietnam
GEOGRAPHIC CODES: ASVT; NNUS
GEOGRAPHIC NAMES: Vietnam; United States
PRODUCT/INDUSTRY NAMES: 3761232 (Communications Satellites); 3662130 (Satellite Communications Eqp); 9103266 (Export Controls-Other)
SIC CODES: 3663 Radio & TV communications equipment
FILE SEGMENT: TI File 148

American businesses bank on: global marketing. (opportunities for U.S.corporations in Vietnam)
Brewer, Geoffrey
Sales & Marketing Management, v146, n4, p15(1)
April, 1994
ISSN: 0163-7517   LANGUAGE: ENGLISH
RECORD TYPE: FULLTEXT; ABSTRACT
WORD COUNT: 493   LINE COUNT: 00041

ABSTRACT: The end of the US embargo against Vietnam that lasted for 19 years was announced by Pres Clinton in Feb 1994. Business-to-business opportunities are particularly appealing since there is a demand for telecommunications and high technology services and products.
SPECIAL FEATURES: illustration; other
INDUSTRY CODES/NAMES: ADV Advertising, Marketing and Public Relations
DESCRIPTORS: Investments, American—Vietnam; Corporations, American—Foreign operations; Telecommunications industry—International trade; High technology industry—International trade; Vietnam—Relations with the United States
PRODUCT/INDUSTRY NAMES: 9103200 (Trade Relations); 4810000 (Telecommunications); 3661000 (Telecommunications Equipment)
SIC CODES: 4800 COMMUNICATION; 4810 Telephone Communication; 3660 Communications Equipment
FILE SEGMENT: MI File 47

Note also that at the bottom of each citation (or "record" in database lingo) there are a variety of indexing codes, called descriptors. These help you see how the database producer has indexed and classified this item, making it easier for you to make your search more precise by using those codes.

Now we can instruct Dialog to show us the fulltext of the first item. Here's what we see:

```
Vietnam: the satcom protocol. (export laws on satellite communi-
nication equipment) (includes related article)
Manuta, Lou
Satellite Communications, v18, n5, p18(2)
May, 1994
ISSN: 0147-7439       LANGUAGE: ENGLISH
RECORD TYPE: FULLTEXT
WORD COUNT:    1337      LINE COUNT:    00113
```

TEXT: The bamboo curtain around Vietnam has opened. A country that lacks a sufficient telecommunications infrastructure and is comprised of over 70 million literate people has just become a nation of 70 million potential consumers of American-made products and services. While some trade barriers remain in place, the nearly 20-year-old embargo against Vietnam was dropped in early 1994.

During past decades, it was impossible to obtain an export license to ship equipment to Vietnam. E today, satellites are subject to United States export control laws.

But these export barriers are falling. The Departments of Commerce and State amended their regulations in September 1993 to transfer communications satellites and other equipment from the U.S. Munitions List to the Commerce Control List, thus relaxing export requirements.

In addition to communications satellites, export will now be permitted for GPS receivers (except if specifically designed for the military), communications satellite components, marketing data, technical data necessary to launch and operate satellites, and passive remote sensing ground stations (unless national security would be jeopardized). Non-military or commercial remote sensing satellites and weather satellites are also expected to be removed from the Munitions List, but military satellites and production data and components for satellites will remain on the List. In addition, the House Foreign Affairs Committee's Subcommittee on Economic Policy, Trade, and Environment passed legislation on a general re-write of the Export Administration Act. The Act, which bases the export of strategic goods, including satellites and satellite components, on criteria dating from the Cold War, is expected to be completely updated in 1994.

(...The text continues)

Another powerful online database search system is called
Nexis, which contains the fulltext of hundreds of newpapers,
magazines, and other information sources. A search on this system turns up several relevant references, among them a management briefing from the Bureau of National Affairs on trade
negotiations between the U.S. and Vietnam. Here's an excerpt
from what we found:

BNA MANAGEMENT BRIEFING

Oct. 4, 1995
LENGTH: 1106 words
BODY:
International Trade
U.S., VIETNAM TO BEGIN NEGOTIATIONS ON BILATERAL TRADE AGREE-
MENT, SPERO SAYS
WASHINGTON (BNA) — The United States and Vietnam will begin to
negotiate a bilateral trade agreement in what is expected to
be a long and complicated negotiation, Undersecretary of State
for Economic, Business, and Agricultural Affairs Joan Spero
said Oct. 3.
    U.S. officials would like to reach a comprehensive trade
agreement with Vietnam as a basis for bilateral economic relations, Spero said at a press briefing. However, she left open
the possibility that the administration could allow U.S. export
financing and investment insurance agencies to operate in
Vietnam before the trade agreement is concluded.
    Senior Vietnamese officials are in Washington and plan to
participate in a conference organized by the U.S.-Vietnam Trade
Forum Oct. 5. Spero met Oct.2 with Vietnamese Minister of Trade
Le Van Triet, she said.
    President Clinton July 11 announced the normalization of
economic ties with Vietnam. Clinton said the United States
would implement U.S. government programs to develop trade with
Vietnam "consistent with U.S. laws."
    Spero praised Vietnam for economic reforms that have
brought it a growth rate averaging around 8 percent over the
last four years. However, the Asian country is "a difficult
place to do business," she added.

"The Vietnamese government restricts the operations of foreign businesses through an array of non-transparent requirements on trade and investment activity," she said.

Vietnam maintains a "highly protective" business and trade regime, Spero said. The Asian nation uses import quotas to shield domestic industries, she said.

❏ PROBLEM 2: DEMOGRAPHICS TO GO

Now you're working for a gourmet coffee retail chain store, and you're planning to expand to some new locations in the Northwest of the United States. You've heard that the small but growing city of Missoula, Montana would be receptive to your line of special coffees, but you need to get some good demographic data to understand the makeup of the region.

Luckily, in the world of online information, one area that's easy to come by is demographic statistics. Many public and university libraries offer CD-ROM access to U.S. census bureau data, and there are many private firms that take census information and reformat it and add supplementary data to make it more useful and easier to use.

One such firm is Market Statistics Inc., whose database called Population Demographics on Dialog offers a great deal of demographic data on regions throughout the country. Here, for example, is a portion of what we found on Missoula, Montana:

```
DIALOG(R)File 581:Population Demographics
(c) 1995 Market Statistics. All rts. reserv.
00035109
Level:          Zip—59801
State:          MT (MONTANA)
County:         MISSOULA
Zip Code:       59801
Census Div:     Mountain
MSA:            (9999)
DMA:            MISSOULA (762)
```

TOTALS & MEDIANS

	1990 Census	1994 Estimate	% Change 90 to 94	1999 Projection
Total Population	32,816	34,758	5.9%	38,550
Total Households	13,391	14,177	5.8%	13,234
Total Household Pop	30,640	32,385	5.7%	36,177
Avg Household Size	2.29	2.28	0.4%	2.73
Avg Household Income	$27,261	$32,847	20.4%	$48,230
Med Household Income	$20,180	$27,159	34.5%	$33,667
Total Families	NA	NA	NA	NA
Per Capita Income	$11,124	$13,397	20.4%	$16,557
Buying Power Index	NA	0.016900	NA	0.018400

POPULATION BY AGE

	1990 Census		1994 Estimate		1999 Projection	
	Number	Percent	Number	Percent	Number	Percent
0-5	2,672	8.1%	2,888	8.3%	2,985	7.7%
6-11	2,357	7.2%	2,476	7.1%	2,872	7.5%
12-17	2,274	6.9%	2,459	7.1%	2,773	7.2%
18-24	5,880	17.9%	5,928	17.1%	6,102	15.8%
25-34	5,753	17.6%	5,660	16.3%	5,687	14.8%
35-44	5,058	15.4%	5,666	16.3%	6,487	16.8%
45-54	2,778	8.5%	3,367	9.7%	4,380	11.4%
55-64	2,045	6.2%	2,061	5.9%	2,445	6.3%
65-74	2,227	6.8%	2,364	6.8%	2,475	6.4%
75+	1,772	5.4%	1,889	5.4%	2,344	6.1%

HOUSEHOLD INCOME

	1990 Census		1994 Estimate		1999 Projection	
	Number	Percent	Number	Percent	Number	Percent
$0-9,999	3,057	22.8%	2,737	19.3%	2,040	15.4%
$10k-14,999	1,965	14.7%	1,822	12.9%	1,440	10.9%
$15k-24,999	2,948	21.9%	2,809	19.7%	2,410	18.2%
$25k-34,999	1,887	14.1%	1,879	13.3%	1,695	12.8%
$35k-49,999	1,884	14.1%	2,107	14.9%	1,929	14.6%
$50k-74,999	1,182	8.8%	1,848	13.0%	2,118	16.0%
$75k-99,999	268	2.0%	557	3.9%	865	6.5%
$100k-149,999	178	1.3%	352	2.5%	632	4.8%
$150,000+	34	0.3%	66	0.5%	105	0.8%

In addition to the above data, this database also provided breakdowns on the citizens' occupation, education, and much more.

❏ PROBLEM 3: PDA FUTURES

Perhaps in this scenario, you have developed a product that would enhance the performance of products in the PDA (personal digital assistant) market, but before committing to going forward, you want to see how well this type of industry is expected to perform in the near future. Industry newsletters are the kind of media that are often filled with such hard to find, "insider" type data. Two of the best sources for locating such valuable publications are NewsNet, which is an online vendor that consists only of trade newsletters, and the Predicasts Newsletter Database on Dialog.

Here's an excerpt from an article we found on the Predicasts Newsletter database:

ARE PDAs READY FOR RETAIL? When Even the Store Manager Says 'Huh?' Maybe It's Time to Rethink the Niche

Wireless Messaging Report July 18, 1995 V. 3   NO. 14
WORD COUNT: 1976
PUBLISHER: BRP Publications

BIS Strategic Decisions defines a PDA as a device designed pri-
marily for communications that runs an operating system such
as Geos or Magic Cap. Bill Ablondi, a market analyst with BIS,
said that such a definition covers devices such as the Sony
Magic Link, the Apple Newton and the Motorola Envoy but
excludes devices such as the Hewlett-Packard HP 200LX or the
Psion Series 3A.

Those latter two are palmtop PCs, which, though they can be
made to communicate, were designed to work as stand-alone PCs
in the palm of the hand. Same goes for the Sharp Wizard and
the newer Sharp Zaurus. Ablondi said that BIS doesn't count
either as a PDA, though both are selling very well. The Zaurus,
with its new AT&T Mail access module, actually is sold by its
manufacturer as a PDA, but Ablondi said that for the present,
its sales are counted in a category besides PDAs.

He said that in spite of the narrow definition BIS uses to
describe PDAs, he expects unit sales to increase nearly 59 percent to 154,000 units in 1995, following a 20 percent jump in
1994. He said sales will almost double in 1996 and again in
1997, as the first marriages between PDAs and personal communications services (PCS) begin to bear fruit.

"We're in the embryonic stages of this marketplace," Ablondi
said. As such, the unit sales have been less than impressive.
For those who were expecting millions of unit shipments in this,
the third year of PDA sales, it has been a disappointment. But
for those who realize that it takes time to build a new category, especially at the retail level, it has been slow but
steady growth.

(...the text continues)

It's worth noting here that Predicasts has created a very
sophisticated method for identifying and searching for information on specific industries and products. The firm uses a hierarchical numerical code that can be use to identify both broad and
narrow industries and products. For example, the following are
Predicasts' codes for a series of products falling under the broad
heading of "machinery":

Machinery except electric=	35
Office and Computing Machines=	357
Computer Auxiliar Equipment=	35732
Special Purpose Terminals=	357328
Automatic Teller Machines-	3573282

By using these cascading codes, you can pinpoint precisely what industry and product you need information about, and then instruct the database to locate articles and reports covering just those items indexed with those specified codes.

This coding system is similar to the Standard Industrial Classification (SIC) code system implemented by the government. It's important that all businesses understand SIC codes and their uses. Every industry is assigned a special hierarchical SIC number, which is based on a company's primary business activities. The first two digits correspond to a major industry group, and the following digits further specify industry subgroups.

Although the SIC code system was originally created by the government for classifying businesses and taking a census, the codes have been widely adopted by non-government information sources, and many major databases index companies and products with SIC codes as well. That's why knowing the SIC system is so important. Predicasts, however, has done even better than the SIC code system by creating the proprietary numbering system shown above.

Most libraries' business divisions will have a copy of the guide to the SIC coding system. To buy your own manual, write to:

Standard Industrial Classification Manual
Superintendent of Documents
US Government Printing Office
Washington DC 20402

The manual lists each SIC number along with the industry it belongs to.

❑ PROBLEM 4: QUICK COMPANY COMPOSITES

An investment portfolio you're evaluating includes the New York Times Company. You've heard that newspapers are having trouble retaining readers; you've also heard that many traditional newspapers are moving into new media ventures to increase revenue. You need information. What is the New York Times Co.' financial position? Are sales increasing? What are the New York Times subsidiaries?

Because public firms are required by law to file a variety of in-depth financial and operating statements with the Securities and Exchange Commission (SEC), it is relatively easy to locate good information on these companies. Private companies are more difficult to find information on—though not impossible—and are discussed under Problem 7 later. There are several sources you can turn to get financial and other information. These include Dun & Bradstreet, and American Business Information (Omaha, Nebraska), both of whom make their information available online.

Another long time supplier of company financial data is Disclosure, which specializes in gathering data filed by public companies with the SEC. A quick search on the Disclosure database turns up a great deal of information derived mostly from the filings the firm must make with the SEC. For example, you can view a balance sheet and income statement (partially illustrated on the following pages), as well as a great deal of other data such as an auditor's statement, names of subsidiaries, revenue segment breakdowns, cash flow, stock and dividend information, financial ratios, lists of officers and directors with titles and renumeration and so forth.

BALANCE SHEET

ANNUAL ASSETS ($000s)

Fiscal Year Ending	12/31/94	12/31/93	12/31/92
Cash	41,419	42,058	118,503
Marketable Securities	NA	NA	NA
Receivables	247,750	264,218	192,233
Inventories	30,545	47,271	51,551
Raw Materials	NA	NA	NA
Work in Progress	NA	NA	NA
Finished Goods	NA	NA	NA
Notes Receivable	NA	NA	NA
Other Current Assets	92,060	139,606	70,491
Total Current Assets	411,774	493,153	432,778
Gross Property, Plant & Eq	1,818,768	1,683,511	1,458,586
Accumulated Depreciation	660,017	571,487	555,831
Net Property, Plant & Eq	1,158,751	1,112,024	902,755
Investment & Adv to Subs	85,433	76,020	139,392
Other Non-Current Assets	NA	NA	NA
Deferred Charges (Asset)	NA	NA	NA
Intangibles	1,379,466	1,420,953	456,223
Deposits & Other Assets	102,207	113,054	63,826
Total Assets	3,137,631	3,215,204	1,994,974

ANNUAL LIABILITIES ($000s)

Fiscal Year Ending	12/31/94	12/31/93	12/31/92
Notes Payable	NA	NA	2,643
Accounts Payable	121,504	177,742	139,115
Current Long Term Debt	NA	NA	NA
Curr Portion of Cap Leases	2,681	2,590	NA
Accrued Expenses	249,350	242,771	137,883
Income Taxes	NA	NA	NA
Other Current Liabilities	77,697	130,627	119,508
Total Current Liabilities	451,232	553,730	399,149
Mortgages	NA	NA	NA
Deferred Charges (Liab)	176,588	196,875	187,701
Convertible Debt	NA	NA	NA
Long Term Debt	473,530	413,581	158,131
Non-Current Capital Leases	49,666	46,482	48,780
Other Long Term Liab	441,323	403,869	199,799
Total Liabilities	1,592,339	1,614,537	993,560
Minority Interest (Liab)	NA	NA	NA
Preferred Stock	1,753	1,784	1,784
Common Stock Net	10,862	10,825	8,862
Capital Surplus	597,860	599,758	164,928
Retained Earnings	1,179,715	1,022,958	1,065,347
Treasury Stock	244,898	34,658	239,507
Other Liabilities	NA	NA	NA
Shareholders Equity	1,545,292	1,600,667	1,001,414
Total Liab & Net Worth	3,137,631	3,215,204	1,994,974

ANNUAL INCOME STATEMENT ($000s)			
Fiscal Year Ending	12/31/94	12/31/93	12/31/92
Net Sales	2,357,563	2,019,654	1,773,535
Cost of Goods	1,262,724	1,136,613	1,004,629
Gross Profit	1,094,839	883,041	768,906
R&D Expenditures	NA	NA	NA
Sell, General & Admin Exp	883,597	756,460	680,498
Income Before Depr & Amort	211,242	126,581	88,408
Depreciation & Amort	NA	NA	NA
Non-Operating Income	200,873	NA	53,768
Interest Expense	28,162	25,375	26,115
Income Before Taxes	383,953	101,206	8,525
Provision for Income Taxes	173,868	43,231	11,079
Minority Interest Income	NA	NA	NA
Investment Gains	NA	NA	NA
Other Income	3,264	51,852	8,718
Net Income Before Ex Items	213,349	6,123	11,272
Ex Items & Discontinued Op	NA	NA	33,437
Net Income	213,349	6,123	44,709
Outst Shares (not in 000s)	97,809,966	106,858,132	79,706,065

Subsidiaries:

AFFILIATED PUBLICATIONS, INC.
*GLOBE NEWSPAPER CO.
*BOSTON GLOBE ELECTRONIC PUBLISHING, INC.
*BOSTON GLOBE INVESTMENTS, INC.
**ZAKREWSKI LTD. PARTNERSHIP, 99%
*COMMUNITY NEWSDEALERS INC.

*GLOBE SPECIALTY PRODUCTS, INC.
**NEW ENGLAND DIRECT, INC.
*RETAIL SALES, INC.
*WILSON TISDALE CO.
COMET-PRESS NEWSPAPERS, INC.
CROSSROADS HOLDING CORP.
CRUISING WORLD PUBLICATIONS, INC.
DONOHUE MALBAIE INC., 49%
FERNADINA BEACH NEWS-LEADER, INC.
GAINESVILLE SUN PUBLISHING CO.
GOLF DIGEST/TENNIS, INC.
GOLF WORLD LTD.
HENDERSONVILLE NEWSPAPER CORP.
INTERNATIONAL HERALD TRIBUNE SA, 50%
LAKE CITY REPORTER, INC.
LAKELAND LEDGER PUBLISHING CORP.
LONDON BUREAU LTD.
NORTHERN SC PAPER CORP., 80%
*MADISON PAPER INDUSTRIES
NYT 1896T, INC.
NYTRNG, INC.
NYT SPECIAL SERVICES, INC.
OCALA STAR-BANNER CORP.
110 FIFTH AVENUE CORP.
RETAIL MAGAZINES MARKETING COMPANY, INC.
*TIME DISTRIBUTION SERVICES, 37%
ROME BUREAU SRL
SARASOTA HERALD-TRIBUNE CO.
SEBRING NEWS-SUN, INC.
DISPATCH PUBLISHING COMPANY, INC.
HOUMA COURIER NEWSPAPER CORP.
LEESBURG DAILY COMMERICAL, INC.
NEW YORK TIMES BROADCASTING SERVICE, INC.
*INTERSTATE BROADCASTING COMPANY, INC.
*TIMES SOUTHWEST BROADCASTING, INC.
NEW YORK TIMES DISTRIBUTION CORP.
NEW YORK TIMES SALES, INC.
NEW YORK TIMES SYNDICATION SALES CORP.
PALATKA DAILY NEWS, INC.
TIMES LEASING, INC.
TIMES ON-LINE SERVICES, INC.

```
TSP NEWSPAPERS, INC.
*TIMES DAILY, INC.
WILMINGTON STAR-NEWS, INC.
WNEP-TV, INC.
```

Note that many public company filings are available for free over the Internet, over a system called EDGAR. For more information, see the section on the Internet later in this book.

❏ PROBLEM 5: LET YOUR KEYBOARD DO THE WALKING

You're preparing for a three-day business trip to a client firm in Pleasant Hill, California. Since you'll be negotiating a contact, you'll need on-the-spot, top quality typing support for contract changes. Time is short and this must be arranged in advance. A search of Dun & Bradstreet's Electronic Business Directory yields a few choices in nearby Concord, two of which are reprinted here. (Fictitious companies have been substituted for the actual company names provided by the search)

```
CUTTING EDGE BUSINESS CENTER
140 MAIN STREET
CONCORD, CA 94523

TELEPHONE: 415-555-1212

COUNTY: CONTRA COSTA
SMSA: 526 (SAN-FRAN-OAKLAND, CA)
REGION: PACIFIC
INDUSTRY GROUP: BUSINESS SERVICES

PRIMARY SIC:
7338        SECRETARIAL AND COURT REPORTING, NSK
73389903    SECRETARIAL AND TYPING SERVICE

THIS IS A(N):
    CORPORATION
    FIRM
    SINGLE LOCATION
```

```
D-U-N-S NUMBER:            11-111-1111
NUMBER OF EMPLOYEES        B (1-4)
COUNTY POPULATION          9 (500,000 AND OVER)


CUTTING EDGE SECRETARIAL SERVICE
140 MAIN STREET
CONCORD, CA 94523


TELEPHONE: 415-555-1212
COUNTY: CONTRA COSTA
SMSA: 526 (SAN-FRAN-OAKLAND, CA)
REGION: PACIFIC
INDUSTRY GROUP: BUSINESS SERVICES


PRIMARY SIC:
7338            SECRETARIAL AND COURT REPORTING, NSK
73389903        SECRETARIAL AND TYPING SERVICE

THIS IS A(N):f
    CORPORATION
    FIRM
    SINGLE LOCATION

D-U-N-S NUMBER:            11-111-1111
NUMBER OF EMPLOYEES        B (1-4)
COUNTY POPULATION          9 (500,000 AND OVER)
```

Note that one of the easiest and fastest ways to find these kinds of directory listings is by using a CD-ROM phone book type directory. Many libraries offer free use of these useful and popular products, which allow you to search the names, addresses, and phone numbers of people and businesses throughout the United States. If your computer has a CD-ROM drive, you can buy one yourself for about $50–$150. (Leading vendors include American Business Information (ABI), ProPhone and PhoneDisc.)

❏ PROBLEM 6: PRODUCT AND INDUSTRY MARKET REPORTS

You're in new business development for a large processed food company that wants to expand its line into low and no fat healthy offerings. You need to determine demand for these kinds of products for a presentation to top management within two weeks. You begin with a short search of the Findex database of market studies that instantly provides abstracts for two such reports:

```
LOW-FAT FOODS SHOPPERS
1993    146 P.    $1200    ONE-TIME
Publ: HealthFocus
PO Box 7174
Des Moines, IA 50309-7174
Phone: 515-274-1307
Fax: 515-274-3117
Contact: Linda Gilbert, President

Availability: PUBLISHER
Document Type: MARKET/INDUSTRY STUDY
```

This report profiles shoppers who always or usually choose low-fat versions of dairy foods, low-fat cereals, and low-fat meats. Provides category specific demographic and attitudinal profiles of all three categories of low-fat foods, including specific health and dietary actions and concerns. Provides an understanding of the differences between low-fat dairy, low-fat cereal, and low-fat meat users, of their eating and shopping habits, and their health and nutrition behavior.
Descriptors: HEALTH & SPECIALTY FOOD; FOOD, DIET; FOOD, EATING HABITS; FOOD, HEALTH.

```
MEAT MARKET FOR HEALTHY PREPARED FOODS
SEP    1995    200+ P.    $2250    ONE-TIME
Publ: FIND/SVP
625 Ave of the Americas
New York, NY 10011
Phone: 212-807-2635
Phone: 800-346-3787
Fax: 212-645-7681
Contact: Joanna Leefer
```

```
Availability: PUBLISHER
Report No.: AA444
Document Type: MARKET/INDUSTRY STUDY
```

This report on the retail market for prepared foods analyzes, quantifies, and projects market size and growth prospects. Covers low-fat and low-cholesterol prepared foods; low-sodium products; high-fiber breads and cereals; and vitamin- and mineral-enriched foods. Provides historical data for the period 1989 through 1994, and forecasts for 1995 through 1999. Reviews the changing consumer environment and evaluates opportunities for food producers and marketers. Provides a review of government regulation of the food industry with particular reference to the new food labeling regulations which went into effect in early May of 1994. Discusses consumer responses to these regulations and evaluates their potentially stimulative impact on the overall market for prepared healthy foods. Examines other key variables including emerging food manufacturing technology, distribution channels, recent acquisitions and mergers, and trends in research and development expenditures and advertising. Profiles important players, including Campbell Soup, ConAgra, J.H. Heinz, RJR Nabisco, Philip Morris Companies, and Quaker Oats. Also profiles smaller niche players which reflect the innovations taking place in the market.
Descriptors: HEALTH & SPECIALTY FOOD; FOOD, HEALTH; FOOD, PROCESSED; FOOD, SPECIALTY; CAMPBELL SOUP; CONAGRA; HEINZ (JH); MORRIS (PHILIP) COS; QUAKER OATS; RJR NABISCO

Note that these abstracts are derived from "off the shelf" market research reports. These studies are written for sale to the general business community, and are typically much less expensive than individually customized studies. If the information contained in a database abstract is not sufficient, you can then directly contact either the database producer or the report publisher to inquire about buying the full report. Reports typically cost anywhere from $2,500-$3,000.

You will probably find that most "off the shelf" studies are quite suitable for your research purposes. Should you determine that you need more customized information, you can then contact a research or survey firm to obtain a price quote.

❑ PROBLEM 7: DETAILS ON A SMALL, PRIVATE FIRM

You're a software developer, and you think that you may have developed a program that will allow users to more efficiently search and filter their electronic news. But before going too much further, you want to find out as much as you can about how other leading players in the market funded themselves and established initial business relationships. From your initial readings, you've discovered that a firm called Individual Inc., out of Cambridge, Massachusetts seems to be the leader.

The problem is, Individual is a small, privately held firm, and is not obligated to reveal its finances or make public filings. How can you find out more about this company?

Luckily, although it is more difficult to find information on privately held firms than public ones, there are sources you can turn to. For example, there are credit reports, which include data on a company's history, operations, credit rating, net worth, and so on. These are available on an on-demand basis from Dun & Bradstreet, (via its D&B Express service) and online from vendors such as NewsNet. Other suppliers of credit reports and company profiles include American Business Information, TRW and GlobalScan, which specializes in international companies. These reports often include a variety of hard-to-find useful data. Dun & Bradstreet reports, for example offer a brief biography of the principals and the size (in square footage) of the office space the firm occupies. Other data provided in credit reports may include the name of the company's bank and accountant, import/export data, sales and employment trends, and more.

Another good source for digging up information on private companies is a database called *Business Dateline*, which culls articles about smaller firms from hundreds of regional and city business publications around the country. These smaller journals typically contain in-depth articles about companies that are making an impact on the community, and may include interviews with the Presidents of these private firms and information unavailable from other sources.

Here's an excerpt from an interview with Individual Inc.'s President Yosi Amram that turned up on a publication called Mass High Tech, located on Business Dateline:

```
Individual's interactive newspaper hits stride
Porter, Patrick L
MASS HIGH TECH (Watertown, MA, US), v12 n3 s1 p2
PUBL DATE: 940124
JOURNAL CODE: MAHT
DOC TYPE: Newspaper article
DATELINE: Cambridge, MA, US          WORD COUNT: 5,015

TEXT:

MHT: What led you to the idea of a personalized interactive
newspaper?

AMRAM: I had started to look at this notion of the knowledge
worker and how one might help them filter  and synthesize infor-
mation. I saw that traditional  on-line databases that are sup-
posed to provide access to information were hard to use and did-
n't really address the end-user needs—even I had been a frus-
trated user of Dialog and Dow Jones News Retrieval. At Aegis we
had looked at making some investments in companies like Delphi
(an on-line service) but we decided not to because we saw that
their market was limited to the PC professional and enthusiast.
```

(...the text continues...)

```
MHT: Where did you get the money?

AMRAM: We raised $100,000 of seed capital, half from my fami-
ly and friends...
MHT: And they're still your friends?

AMRAM: (laughing) Yes. A lot of people advised me not to do
that because of the risk of destroying  those relationships,
but luckily it worked out okay. Also, I ran across Ed
Fredkin...

MHT: That name sounds very familiar.

AMRAM: He's fairly well known in the Boston high-tech commu-
nity now but he was a college dropout of  Cal Tech and start-
```

ed a company called Information International in the '60s that was building computer pre-press systems and color separations for newspapers. He took that public and sold the company and then went to MIT and actually built their computer science department and lab. Even though he was a college dropout he was the director of lab at computer science. He and Minsky built the AI Lab at MIT. He was interested in the concept because it could mine computer-based intelligence and publishing—two angles of what he's done. So he invested $50,000 and gave us an office and helped us get off the ground.we were able to secure some additional venture capital.

MHT: From whom?

AMRAM: The first two professional venture firms were Grace Ventures and Venture Capital Fund of New England. We also brought in some additional private investors who were successful entrepreneurs in the Boston area, Mort Goulder who was a founder of Sanders, and Andy Devereaux, one of the founders of American Cable Systems which later was sold to Continental Cablevision, and Ted Johnson, one of the early employees at Digital Equipment. He built their sales and marketing department. So it was a combination of professional venture investors as well as some successful entrepreneurs. We raised about $1 million. That was at the end of '89. Then we rolled out the service in 1990.

(the text continues...)

MHT: Is there a gigantic mainframe chewing through this?

(...the text continues...)

MHT: We've talked about sources. Now about customers? Who they are? Why do they use it?

AMRAM: We have customers across a range of industries. We started out focusing on the information technology industry as a vertical but we've rolled out into telecommunications, health care, energy, defense, automotive and financial services. So there are a number of industries. They tend to be information intensive industries where there is a rapid rate of change. They tend to be both in sales and marketing, product develop-

ment, strategic planning and in some cases purchasing. And they
tend to use it for different applications. The competitive
analysis type people and the marketing people tend to use it to
track an industry or their competition. The sales people tend
to use it to track their customers. If a customer opens a new
plant or announces an expansion or layoffs or whatever, the
sales person is attuned to the opportunities and problems in
that client base. The purchasing departments use it to track
vendors so if a vendor announces bankruptcy or gets in financial trouble, they know to watch out. Similarly in banking we've
got loan officers and risk management officers using it to track
their portfolio. So from a credit-watch point of view, if you're
working for Fleet Bank you might track your major customers and
their industries.

   We also deliver Heads Up via wireless. In that environment
it's a mobile executive who is using it to stay in touch while
they're on the road.

(...the text continues)

MHT: Tell me about the Dialog relationship.

AMRAM: Basically there are three sides to the relationship.
They invested in the company and are providing us some capital. The second side is we are going to take some of the databases that they have already gathered and use them. While we
are continually increasing our source pool, they have a large
number of databases and by working with them we can have access
to a lot of sources that we will deliver to our customers
through First and Heads Up. And thirdly we will be developing
some new products that they can market to their audience based
on our existing technologies and some extensions that we're
working on with them. So those are the three aspects of the
relationship. But fundamentally they recognize that they have
this massive database of information but the technology they
have and the model they have is not going to let them get into
the broad audience of professional knowledge workers. We are
working to marry our technology with the deep pool of sources
they have to reach that audience. In addition, they have a
large sales, marketing and distribution force that we want to
leverage. So it's a nice synergy. They approached us this
spring.

COPYRIGHT: Copyright Mass Tech Times Inc. 1994

As you can see, this is highly substantive information that could prove to be invaluable in your research of this small but fast growing industry and current market leaders.

❑ PROBLEM 8: EDUCATING YOUR WORKERS ABOUT AIDS

You know that the workplace in the 90s is a complicated place, and that one of the most difficult issues is sensitively handling difficult personnel issues such as educating staff about AIDS. You know you're not the first company that's going to have to come to grips with this issue, so you don't want to reinvent the wheel.

What have other firms done here? What works and what doesn't work? You want to take a quick scan on what leading companies are doing. A top-notch management database called ABI/INFORM comes to the rescue with a handful of on-the-mark summaries and abstracts.

Employee education programs replace fears about AIDS with facts
Tomlinson, Janice
HRMagazine   v40n5   PP: 99-102   May 1995 CODEN: PEADAY   ISSN: 1047-3149
JRNL CODE: PAD
DOC TYPE: Journal article   LANGUAGE: English   LENGTH: 4 Pages
AVAILABILITY: Fulltext   online.   Photocopy   available   from ABI/INFORM 6437.01
WORD COUNT: 1628

ABSTRACT: Employers must create an environment that allows employees with AIDS or HIV to contribute for as long as they are physically able. At Chubb & Son Inc., there has never been an instance of insurmountable resistance to work with a colleague diagnosed with AIDS. The company attributes its successful track record to 2 things: Chubb's corporate culture and commitment to providing AIDS awareness education to all employees. Employee education can create an environment that encourages open, honest communication about AIDS and support for employees who contract the disease. Providing this education is not only the right to do, it also makes good business sense.

COMPANY NAMES:
Chubb & Son Inc
GEOGRAPHIC NAMES: US
DESCRIPTORS: Case studies; Insurance industry; AIDS; Human resources; Employee relations programs; Education
CLASSIFICATION CODES: 9190 (CN=United States); 9110 (CN=Company specific); 8200 (CN=Insurance industry); 6100 (CN=Human resource planning)

Setting policy is the best policy: Tackling AIDS, HIV in workplace
Anonymous
Nation's Restaurant News v29n16 PP: 33 Apr 17, 1995 ISSN: 0028-0518
JRNL CODE: NRN
DOC TYPE: Journal article LANGUAGE: English LENGTH: 1 Pages
AVAILABILITY: Fulltext online. Photocopy available from ABI/INFORM
WORD COUNT: 566

ABSTRACT: Daka International and Marriott Management Services are among the large employers being recognized for taking proactive stands related to AIDS education and dealing with HIV-infected workers. An editorial commends these companies for talking about AIDS, as courageous dialogue and the sharing of ideas can make a difference in terms of reducing the carnage inflicted by HIV.

GEOGRAPHIC NAMES: US
DESCRIPTORS: AIDS; Restaurants; Education; Personnel policies
CLASSIFICATION CODES: 8380 (CN=Hotels & restaurants); 6100 (CN=Human resource planning); 9190 (CN=United States); 9000 (CN=Short Article)
AIDS in the workplace: An executive update Executive summary
Stone, Romuald A; Hornstein, Henry A; Donahue, Mary Ann; Lashutka, Serge
Academy of Management Executive v8n3 PP: 52-64 Aug 1994 ISSN: 0896-3789
JRNL CODE: AEX
DOC TYPE: Journal article LANGUAGE: English LENGTH: 13 Pages
SPECIAL FEATURE: References
AVAILABILITY: Fulltext online. Photocopy available from ABI/INFORM 16369.01
Article Ref. No.: B-AEX-31-3
WORD COUNT: 7107

ABSTRACT: It is estimated that one million Americans, or one in 250, is currently infected with the human immunodeficiency virus (HIV). Leaders at all levels of government and business need to be keenly concerned about HIV and the acquired immunodeficiency syndrome (AIDS). The HIV/AIDS pandemic is a health disaster that threatens and affects everyone. It is an epidemic, deadly disease that is not yet under control and for which there is no cure or vaccine. Recently concluding its 4-year assignment to advise the US on issues and needs related to the AIDS epidemic, the National Commission on AIDS suggests that if the disease is to be conquered, then strong, positive leadership is required to overcome ignorance and fear, as well as to rectify the serious flaws and deficits in care and prevention strategies. Unfortunately, too many executives want to treat this alarm as yesterday's news. The lifetime AIDS-related medical care for a person with AIDS is estimated to run from $70,000 to $100,000. After the first symptoms of AIDS become apparent, the patient's lifetime averages about 24 months.

COMPANY NAMES:
National Commission on AIDS
Sun Life Assurance Co of Canada (DUNS:20-726-3773)
Polaroid Corp (DUNS:00-134-4373 TICKER:PRD)
Honeywell Inc (DUNS:00-132-5240 TICKER:HON)
Levi Strauss & Co (DUNS:00-910-9273)
GEOGRAPHIC NAMES: US
DESCRIPTORS: AIDS; Personnel policies; Social responsibility; Federal legislation; Education; Social policy
CLASSIFICATION CODES: 9190 (CN=United States); 1200 (CN=Social policy); 6100 (CN=Human resource planning); 4320 (CN=Legislation); 6200 (CN=Training & development)

Business responds to AIDS
Romano, Catherine
Management Review v83n3 PP: 5 Mar 1994 CODEN: MRVWDJ ISSN: 0025-1895
JRNL CODE: MRV
DOC TYPE: Journal article
LANGUAGE: English
LENGTH: 1 Pages
AVAILABILITY: Fulltext online. Photocopy available from ABI/INFORM 340.00
Article Ref. No.: B-MRV-88-3
WORD COUNT: 266

ABSTRACT: The Centers for Disease Control and Prevention (CDC) and a public/private partnership of health organizations, labor and management have created the Business Responds to AIDS (BRTA) program to assist businesses in forming comprehensive HIV and AIDS programs. The program was spurred by the fact that one in 250 Americans is infected with AIDS, and only around 20% of US companies have AIDS-related policies.

GEOGRAPHIC NAMES: US
DESCRIPTORS: AIDS; Employee assistance programs; Personnel policies; Associations
CLASSIFICATION CODES: 9000 (CN=Short Article); 9190 (CN=United States); 9540 (CN=Nonprofit institutions); 6100 (CN=Human resource planning)

Note that in these searches, the data is presented in what's called straight ascii text: that is, there are no graphics or illustrations reproduced from the original journal article or item.

As of late 1995, this straight ascii format was still largely the standard, but this is changing quickly, and it's expected that within the next couple of years, the technology will be perfected so that online printouts will more often be replicas of the original items, including all the original formatting. This makes printouts much more attractive, and makes reading them much easier. A few database vendors are already moving in this direction, including Profound, UMI, and DataTimes (EyeQ), which, as discussed earlier, are gearing their business online systems not to information professionals, but to individual businesspersons.

There are countless other questions that databases can answer. For example:

Need to find demographic data on a segment of the population? Try *Cendata*, the database of the United States Bureau of the Census.

Curious to see if the government has published anything of interest recently? *GPO Monthly Catalog* will describe the latest reports.

Want to read what the major dailies have written about the latest political developments? Check the *Newspaper & Periodical Abstracts*.

Need to check some facts on a patent filed by a competitor? Just go online with *United States Patent Abstracts* or *Derwent's World Patents Index (WPI)*.

Like to find out if there are any conferences coming up in your industry? Take a look at *Eventline*.

Want to fill in your upcoming speech with some pithy quotations? Check the *Quotations Database*.

Planning on investing in a new technology, and want to know what the think tanks think of its future? Search *Arthur D. Little/Online*.

Need facts on genetic engineering? Search *Derwent Biotechnology Abstracts*.

Trying to find an obscure book published in England? Search *British Books in Print*.

Wondering how the public feels about environmental issues? Find out by searching *Public Opinion Online*.

Looking for a journal on the subject of virtual reality? Check *Ulrich's International Periodicals Directory*.

Trying to find out what Japan is working on these days? Search the *Japan Economic Newswire Plus* database.

Want to read press releases issued by companies announcing their new products? Search *PR Newswire* or *Businesswire*.

Trying to dig out the facts behind a news development in the computer industry? Check the *Computer Database*.

And, if you're wondering whether your boss really suffers from a paranoid personality or is merely neurotic, you can check *Mental Health Abstracts*.

Speaking of individuals you may want to check out, there are a variety of databases like *Information America People Finder* and *CDB Infotek* that allow searching for data on individuals, including addresses and social security numbers—even vehicle ownership (including yachts and aircraft) and driving records.

In addition, databases exist that allow significant legal research on both open and concluded cases, as well as bankruptcies, liens, and judgements.

Leading Business Databases

Of course, a listing like the one above could be virtually endless. In other words, if you have a question—any question—there's a reasonably good chance that there is an online database available to help you find the answer. The following is a sample of leading business databases, and the kind of information each provides:

• *ABI/Inform.* This database scans 800 primary business publications and provides information on all phases of management and administration, applicable to many types of businesses and industries.

• *Business Dateline.* This database contains the full text of articles from over 350 regional business publications throughout the United States and Canada. Articles cover regional business activities and trends, information about small companies, new start-ups, family-owned and closely-held firms, their products or services, and the executives who run them.

• *Claims/United States Patent Abstracts.* This database contains patents listed in the general, chemical, electrical, and mechanical sections of the *Official Gazette of the United States Patent and Trademark Office.* It offers information from as far back as 1950 for chemical patents, 1963 for electrical and mechanical patents, and 1980 for design patents.

• *Disclosure.* This database provides in-depth financial information on over 11,000 companies. The information is derived from reports filed with the United States Securities and Exchange Commission by publicly-owned firms. Extracts of 10-K and 10-Q financial reports are among those available.

• *Dow Jones News.* This service reports up-to-the-minute news on business and finance worldwide as transmitted through the Dow Jones News Service. It provides coverage as current as thirty seconds and as far back as ninety days. A companion database contains a library of all past articles in the *Wall Street Journal* and *Barron's*.

• *Dun's Market Identifiers.* This database provides detailed information on over 10 million United States public and private companies, including address, product, and financial and marketing information.

• *Investext.* This database is comprised of more than 250,000 full-text company and industry reports and analyses, written by over 1,000 financial analysts from over 200 investment banks and research firms worldwide. Coverage includes 14,000 companies worldwide and 53 industry groups.

• *Nexis.* Actually more then a single database, Nexis is an entire online database search system which provides the complete text of hundreds of newspapers as well as many top trade journals and publications. It is considered one of the most powerful of the online database systems, and is used by many professional researchers and company librarians.

• *PR Newswire.* This database provides the complete text of news releases prepared by companies, public relations agencies, trade associations, governmental agencies, and other sources. The file is updated on a continuous basis. A competitor to PR Newswire which specializes a little more in high technology news is Business Wire.

• *PROMT.* This database provides abstracts and full-text records from over hundreds of publications around the world. It specializes in providing hard data on subjects like market size and shares, trends, mergers and acquisitions, research and development, new products and technologies, sales and consumption, and much more.

• *Reuter Textline.* This database contains abstracts, citations, and, in most cases, the complete text of articles appearing in hundreds of the world's major daily and financial newspapers and journals.

• *Trade and Industry Index.* This database provides current and comprehensive coverage of business and trade news from over 1,000 trade journals and industry-related periodicals.

Where and How You Can Perform a Search

When it comes to performing a database search, you have a few options. One is to do the search yourself on your own computer. All you need is a modem and communications software. Then you can "sign up" with one of the online database hosts (or with a database producer directly), learn that vendor's command and search protocols, and get started.

A few words of caution are in order if you plan on doing searches yourself. Conducting good database searches is a skill—and a bit of an art—and if you are not experienced, you might not obtain useful results. For example, if your search is too narrowly focused, you may not get any results; if it's too broad, you will be swamped with too much data. If you are imprecise or do not understand the specific rules of the database you are searching, you can easily get irrelevant and useless information. That's why it is so important to read carefully all the search instructions that the online host provides, call any "help" lines for assistance, and attend training sessions that hosts offer to their users. The time you spend learning these systems is well spent, considering the cost of conducting online searches and the importance of getting the right information!

Remember this: computer searching can be costly! Since searching professional databases typically costs from $50 to over $100 per hour, it's easy to see how expensive searching can become, even if you do just a few short searches every week.

It is true, though, that since this book was lasted updated in 1993, several database producers have developed powerful search systems that are geared for non-professional users or what the industry calls the "business end-user." These systems are graphically based, don't require knowledge of Boolean search techniques, and are typically less expensive to search then professional online services. The following are the most notable of these:

• Profound Inc. (New York, NY)
Profound offers in-depth business news, market reports, coun-

try studies, company backgrounds and stock quotes in full graphical format and is geared to nonprofessional searchers

• EyeQ (DataTimes, Oklahoma City, OK)
For just $39 per month, and $3 per full-text article, users of EyeQ can search high level business databases such as PROMT over a Windows-based graphical interface.

• UMI ProQuest Direct (Ann Arbor, MI)
Another Windows-based search system, this one offers what it calls "manipulable images" that allow you to view articles and items as they originally appeared in print, with photographs, tables, and other graphical materials.

• Reuters New Media (New York, NY)
The parent firm of the well known international newswire has introduced a search system called Business Briefing that combines the power of traditional index codes with an easy point and click system to provide fast and comprehensive access to a vast database of international news and company information.

In addition to the above, there are the slew of the new customized desktop news delivery services, such as NewsPage (Individual Inc, Burlington, MA) and Hoover, (Sandpoint Inc, Cambridge, MA) and others. Using these services requires even less knowledge than searching business end-user systems. Here, all you typically need to do is just check off from a list of subject areas, companies, and industries that are of interest to you. These customized news delivery systems will then automatically and continuously search a wide variety of electronic news sources and databases for items matching your news profile, and deliver the results to you each day directly over your PC.

These search systems are geared to ordinary businesspeople, and are a fast growing industry. They present new opportunities for you to do your own searching and electronic research, and to do so more easily and less expensively then you could have in the past. Keep in mind, though, that because these systems have been simplified, they are sometimes less flexible and less sophisticated than traditional online search services. This may mean that sometimes a search done on these systems is not as precise or as comprehensive as it would have been if performed on a traditional professional online service. This is especially true for the customized news delivery services, which rely heavily on automated AI-type assumptions to make their decisions about what kind of articles and news items are most relevant to your needs, which can often be quite imperfect.

For these reasons, we advise you to use these services carefully, and be particularly aware of each system's scope of coverage and search limitations. If you work for a large organization, we highly recommend seeking out your firm's librarian or information specialist for assistance and advice, as these people are specifically trained and skilled in using search systems.

Because conducting computer searches can be fairly complex, some businesses choose not to do database searches themselves, but instead hire an expert to do searches for them. One option available is to hire an information-finding firm.

❑ INFORMATION-FINDING FIRMS

As discussed in Chapter 4, information-finding firms are trained in conducting searches. They charge you their direct cost to do the search, as well as a fee (usually an hourly rate). The advantage of this option is that you don't pay any fixed costs or worry about training, and you do not need access to a large number of different databases. Furthermore, most such firms retain highly proficient searchers and usually offer related research services. You need to be a bit careful when choosing an information-finding company, as abilities, expertise, and prices vary widely. Ask the firm you are considering these key questions:

• How long have you been performing online searches?

• How many searches have you conducted in my particular area of inquiry?

• Which databases and online vendors will you be using, and why?

• Who will actually conduct the search? What is their background and experience?

The best firms will spend a good deal of time with you before doing the search, asking *you* key questions, such as: What kind of information do you need? Why do you need it? What will you be doing with it? Have you found anything so far? All of these questions assist the searcher in making a more precise search, and increase the odds that he or she will find the information you seek. To find the names and specific services of information-finding firms, check *Burwell's World Directory of Information Brokers*. This book is available from Burwell Enterprises, 3724 FM 1960 West, Suite 214, Houston, TX 77068; (713) 537–9051.

Another point to keep in mind is that there's often a lot more to finding an answer than a simple online search. Many questions business people have cannot be answered online, and require other forms of research. So you'll want to ask the firm you are considering about their non-online research capabilities and expertise. At FIND/SVP, for example, we have human resources consultants, accountants, legal research experts, technology specialists and international information specialists to handle a wide variety of management concerns and problems.

Which Option Should You Choose?

What's the best option for businesses: doing searches yourself or hiring an expert to do it? Well, as you might expect, the answer is, "It depends."

If you think you will be doing searches fairly regularly—say six times a month or more—it really would pay to have someone on your staff obtain skills and training in online searching. It can also make sense to do searches in-house if you plan on using just a single specialized database in which you can become very proficient. But if you expect to be an infrequent searcher, or plan on searching many different databases or database hosts, you may want to hire an expert—though it still can't hurt to have someone on your staff who knows at least something about online searches. Many companies use both their own searchers and outside information-finding firms. They use their own terminals for frequently searched databases, and ask the specialists to search databases not directly accessed or frequently used.

Potential Pitfalls of Using Online Databases

So far we've talked mainly about the benefits and power of online databases. But there are some pitfalls and potential drawbacks that need to be discussed as well.

We've already talked about how important it is that the searcher be skilled. This point is worth reiterating—a bad search won't retrieve what you want! So be sure that either you, someone on your staff, or someone you hire knows the ins and outs of online searching. One of the major pitfalls of database searching is assuming that because you came up with something from a computer, you have obtained the best information available.

There are a few other important cautions worth passing along. Once you get "hooked" on doing online searches, it's easy to forget that online databases don't contain *everything*, nor are they necessarily the best choice for every information search. Even though online databases contain enormous amounts of information, there are still mountains of data *not* online. These may include scientific and technical reference books, certain government documents, company financials, specialized trade journals, social science research, and so on.

The temptation is to believe that if it can't be found in an online database, then the information does not exist. A very faulty assumption! It *may* be that the information does not exist, but it may also be that it simply is not on any database. Don't forget that, depending on the question, non-online sources can sometimes still be the fastest, cheapest, and most efficient way to go. Say, for example, you need the populations of the top ten cities in Kenya, and you can't find anything online. How about checking that nice set of encyclopedias sitting on your shelf? Also, keep in mind when searching databases that when you retrieve article summaries, or "abstracts," there may be some details and facts omitted from the complete article that would have been useful to you!

Another temptation is to assume that online information must be true. Nonsense! Information obtained from an online database is at least as likely to contain errors, omissions, and unreliable data as any "old-fashioned" source like a newspaper or magazine article. Online information is (typically) just ordinary printed data that has been entered onto a computer database. In fact, sometimes that additional step of keying in the data makes it even more likely that there will be errors!

To help insure that the data you obtain is accurate and reliable, you can take some "pro-active" steps. One is to become very proficient yourself at searching the specific databases you utilize most often. As you get intimately familiar with a database, you are more likely to spot errors and problems. You should also strive to get a second opinion—in other words, check a second or third source to confirm the information. Also, make sure you obtain key details on the databases that reflect on their overall reliability and usefulness—make sure you know when the database was last updated, how much of the database was updated, and what time frame it covers (e.g., reports from July 1991 to September 1995, etc.).

What about searching CD-ROMs? CD-ROMs offer certain advantages over online databases; for example, the ability to budget a fixed cost for the purchase of the disc (as opposed to paying an hourly online rate), and the ease of simply switching on the computer at your own convenience to perform a search.

Another advantage to CD-ROMs is that some systems are capable of reproducing the original articles, including all the graphics and other original page layout elements. This makes for much easier reading of the full-text material. For example, UMI sells a CD-ROM system called *Business Periodicals on Disc*, which contains thousands of business articles. Users can search and then print out an identical copy of the original pages—

including charts, bold print, design, and all the other original design elements.

One particularly nice thing about doing searches on a CD-ROM, is that often you can do so absolutely free! Virtually all academic libraries, and an increasing number of public libraries make CD-ROMs available for patrons to search at absolutely no charge. Your best bet is to go to the largest college or university library in your area, and ask where the business-oriented CD-ROM workstations are located. (Some of the best and most useful CD-ROMs to look for include *ABI/Inform, The Business Index, The Academic Index, Investext,* and *Disclosure*). You shouldn't have to worry about being permitted to use these systems: although if you're not associated with the library you won't be able to check anything out, most academic libraries allow anyone to come in and use the CD-ROM systems.

The major drawback to searching a database on a CD-ROM, compared to online, is that online databases can be updated much more frequently: weekly, daily, even hourly or every few minutes. CD-ROMs, in contrast, are typically updated only on a monthly basis, and sometimes much less frequently. In addition, online providers store a much greater amount of information on their mainframe computers.

What Does the Future Hold for Databases?

Databases, and the online industry, are going through some major changes. Once the province of the technically trained information professional and scientist, online databases have never been simple to learn or geared to the needs of the untrained user. But the recent popularity of CD-ROMs, the Internet, and PCs in general have made online database searching a more popular, consumer-oriented activity. This has put pressure on the database vendors to make their systems easier to use and not so confusingly priced.

The most recent generation of online databases is reflecting this: they are not command driven, but graphically-based (i.e. using icons, graphics, and windows like the operating software of Macintosh or Microsoft's Windows), work via mouse points and clicks, and offer flat rate pricing, rather than the confusing and unpopular "ticking clock," where users are charged for each minute they spend online.

Another development has been the replacement of the traditional Boolean method of searching. This kind of searching uses the "operators" AND, OR, and NOT as the means to more precisely target the kind of information needed. For example, if you were looking for journal articles on importing jewelry from New Zealand or Australia, you'd create a search statement such as: "exporting AND (New Zealand or Australia) AND Jewelry.

Although Boolean searching is a very precise way to target information in a database, it has been losing ground to other search techniques that do not require the user to know the intricacies of proper Boolean searching, and may even, in fact, improve the relevancy of the items retrieved. The latest approach employs search engines that utilize "relevancy ranking" technologies, which take the keywords input by the user, and then examine the frequency and placement of those words in the items searched. The user then receives a listing of those items with the highest ranked score.

The trend is also to offer full image databases, and less expensive pricing. Traditional database vendors are feeling pressure from the free and cheap information available over the Internet, and it's expected that they will need to further reduce their own charges to remain competitive.

8

The Internet

During the last few years, you probably haven't been able to pick up a newspaper or magazine without reading some breathless prose about the explosion of the Internet and its profound impact on all aspects of human endeavors.

One of the more dramatic statements, for example, comes from a prominent observer of the electronic information arena, John Perry Barlow President of the Electronic Frontier Foundation. He's gone so far as to say that although he once thought that the Internet was going to have the greatest impact on humanity since Gutenberg's printing press; he's changed his mind. Now he's certain that it will prove to be the most important development since the discovery of fire.

The most important development since fire—now that's pretty important! While a claim like this may seem so outlandish as to be laughable, there are a lot of thoughtful and knowledgeable people who are saying pretty much the same thing: the Internet is going to change everything.

In what seems like no time, the Internet has grown from an arcane, technical computer network to a mass cultural phenomena, appearing on the cover of *Time* magazine and discussed by everyone from grade school children to members of U.S. congress. And all of this, too, has occurred in a breathtakingly short amount of time. Before 1993, almost nobody had heard of the Internet—but by 1994, almost everybody had.

If you're still unsure exactly what the Internet is, (and if you are, don't worry: a lot more people are still confused about the Internet than you might expect) and why it is engendering such excitement, let's do a very mini-primer here, just to give you some basics.

A Basic Description

The Internet is a conglomeration of electronic computer networks linked around the world: a network of networks. For example, just like the office that you work in might have its computers linked by cables so you can send e-mail and communicate with your colleagues, the Internet also consists of linked computers—but millions of them via telephone lines and modems, and from around the world! As of late 1995, the Internet connected about 30 million people around the globe; that's up from about 4 million in early 1993.

A bit of background: the Internet was begun in 1969 by the Department of Defense as a way to maintain internal communications among the military even under the conditions of a nuclear attack. Over the next decade or so, the Internet grew in size and scope, and eventually became a publicly-run network used for broader public purposes, such as fostering study and communication in education, research, and academia. Until the early 1990s, Internet use was informally restricted to persons associated with an academic or research institution already linked to the network. But as word of the Internet spread, more users hooked into it, there was more casual use, and, significantly, more commercial use too. By the end of 1994, the Internet had become available to just about everyone—including business and commerce.

Today the Internet is used for a wide variety of purposes: the primary ones are sending and receiving electronic mail; discussing and debating issues of common interest in special electronic discussion groups called "newsgroups" and "listservs"; looking for facts and data made available by governments, universities, private companies, and private individuals; reading electronic journals and electronic editions of daily newspapers; searching card catalogs from libraries around the globe; buying and selling products in electronic malls and on company "home pages," and just having fun browsing entertaining sites, looking at lively graphics, and fooling around. One of the unusual aspects of the Internet is that it is not "owned" by any one entity: nobody runs it and there is no centralized authority.

The hottest and fastest growing part of the Internet is the world wide web or just "the web." These are interconnected documents and sites on the Internet you can link to that not only provide text, but also have graphics, sound, color, and often other multimedia. In addition, world wide web sites allow you to instantly "surf" associated web sites that are linked to that site simply by pointing and clicking to where you want to go.

The world wide web is accessed by the use of a software program called a "browser." There are a variety of different browsers available from several different sources; a powerful and popular one that represents the current industry standard is called Netscape. However, a competing standard is a newer browser called Java, which has even more sophisticated capabilities than Netscape.

Just a couple more basics. You can obtain access to the Internet either by signing up with one of the consumer online firms (e.g. America Online, CompuServe, etc.) or by signing up with one of the many private stand-alone Internet service provider (ISPs) around the country. Check your yellow pages or browse a recent newsstand issue of a computer magazine like *PC World* to find names of some providers. If you sign up with one of these companies, you'll typically pay about $15-$25 per month for unlimited use, including e-mail, access to the world wide web, and other Internet functions.

Once you have access, using the Internet doesn't cost anything, although there are certain privately operated sites that charge a fee. Early in its history, there were virtually no Internet sites that charged a fee; but as the net grew, and private firms were allowed to set up shop alongside everyone else, those private entities were permitted to charge users for access to their product or service. The majority of what you'll find on the Internet today is free, but expect an increase in sites that will charge for access to some or all of their content.

The other basic matter you should know about the Internet is how information is organized on the Internet and the function available to access that information. The traditional primary functions and access methods have been via:

• gopher: for browsing menus of information, organized hierarchically

• telnet: to connect to a remote computer on the Internet as if it were locally accessible

• ftp: to download information from a remote computer on the Internet

Note, though, that those above methods for locating and accessing information on the Internet are largely being replaced by the more user-friendly environment of the world wide web.

Each web site (as well as other kinds of Internet sites) are assigned a unique address code called a Uniform Resource Locator (URL). URLs enable Internet users to locate and link directly to a specific site. All URL's begin with the prefix "http://" which is then usually followed by "www" and then a string of letters or numbers. For example, the URL for FIND/SVP's web page is: http://www.findsvp.com. So to link directly to the FIND/SVP page, you would simply enter that code in the appropriate section of your web browser or your Internet service provider's software. (Turn to the next page to see the FIND/SVP web site.)

The two most popular uses of the Internet, after sending electronic mail, are participating in electronic discussion groups, which cover thousands of topics, and "surfing" the world wide web.

Electronic discussion groups, which in Internet lingo are called "usenet" discussion groups and "listserv" mailing lists,

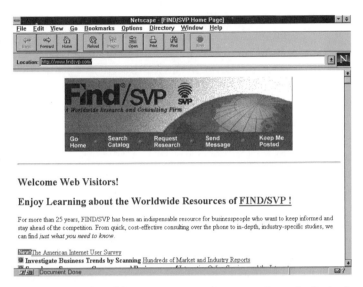

Our firm, Find/SVP, has, like many companies, created a web site to describe and promote what we do as well as offer free information to Internet users. Our address on the web is: http://www.findsvp.com.

allow Internet users from around the globe to communicate and discuss topics of mutual interest. And these topic, span virtually all areas of human activity and interest, ranging from aerospace and ant farms to yodeling and Zaire's economy.

Individuals, governments, businesses, or any person or entity with access to the Internet can set up their own web site and make whatever information or graphical displays they wish available to other Internet users. A web site has its own unique "address" that Internet users enter to link their computer to that site, and upon connecting to a web site, the user first "arrives" at the site's "home page" which is the introduction to the site, and usually contains greetings, an explanation of the purpose of the site, who has created it, and what the site contains.

Like everything else on the Internet, the types of web pages that one can find are really a microcosm of the world at large. Web sites run the gamut from a silly limerick with illustrations to a serious analysis and photographic display of the plight of a forgotten refugee group. They may be created by groups as diverse as the new age or the far right and be as practical as a searchable database of national job listings or as theoretical as a speculative presentation about life on other planets. You can find web sites ranging from a "how I spent my summer vacation" essay by a precocious 12 year old to an advertisement from the IBM Corporation.

From a business perspective, the world wide web presents a wide range of new possibilities. In addition to performing research on the web (covered below), many businesses are setting up home pages as a way to promote or sell their products and services, and offer wider methods of customer assistance. There are about 1,000 pages worth of information that we could continue to tell you about the web and the Internet in general, but an entire overview of the net is beyond the scope of this book. There are literally hundreds of good books available on what to do on the Internet and how to do it. Check the "computers" section of any bookstore to browse through a few and pick one that appeals to you the most. (One early classic we might recommend that's geared specifically for businesspersons is Mary J. Cronin's *Doing Business on the Internet* [Van Nostrand]).

The Internet and the Information Savvy Businessperson

When it comes to anything having to do with the Internet, there's obviously tons of hype. But along with that hype, there are some genuine benefits available to the information savvy businessperson. The two primary ones are performing non-traditional low cost research and finding experts. The two overlap, but we can look at them separately.

❏ RESEARCH

There's good news and bad news about research on the Internet. The good news is that there is a lot of free, cheap, and readily available information, covering a huge range of topics. It's, impossible to generalize on what you can find on the Internet: it would be like explaining what you could find out from the holdings in the world's 100 largest libraries. Suffice it to say, that virtually all topics of human endeavor are there—from gross jokes to great philosophical theories, from fine cuisine recipes to recipes for bomb making. Like Alice's restaurant, you can get anything you want, on the Internet.

The bad news is that, like Woody Allen's ironic metaphor of life as bad restaurant food: (awful...and not enough of it) information on the Internet is often trivial, of dubious reliability, unenlightening—and hard to find!

One of the reasons that the quality of the information on the Internet is so variable, is that unlike, for example, traditional published journals or data on online databases, information posted on the Internet need not pass any scrutiny whatsoever. Anything goes. Everyone from high school sophomores to Nobel prize winning physicists can and do publish their work on the Internet. So there is an enormous amount of "noise" on the net, not found on the professional or consumer online information sources. Databases on these traditional services obtain their data from well-known sources, such as popular and trade magazines, newswires, market research analyst firms, and other mainstream repositories of knowledge.

And, although there are various methods for searching the Internet (more on this later), the net is so vast and decentralized that the techniques that have been developed for research are generally far less precise than what can be done when searching across traditional databases.

Keep in mind too, that searching for information on the Internet, while often kind of fun, can also be very time consuming, especially if you are searching over the world wide web. On the web, depending on the amount of graphics at a site, speed of your connection, and other factors, it can take up to a couple of minutes just to access a single web page! You typically do not search the Internet when you are in a big hurry to find information!

Does this mean, then, that the Internet cannot be a legitimate business research tool? No, what it does mean is that it is not a traditional business research tool. You would not, for example, normally go to the Internet when you are in a hurry to get some well organized article or report to answer a precise business research question, such as "which pharmaceutical firms have the largest market share of the biotechnology industry?" A precisely worded question like that would most likely be most efficiently searched on a traditional business database like *PROMT*, *ABI/Inform*, *Trade & Industry Index*, or *Investext* on one of the major online services like Dialog or Lexis-Nexis.

But if your research on biotechnology was somewhat broader or more flexible, or you just wanted to start learning about the topic, the Internet could be a legitimate tool in your research arsenal—though still not at the expense of searching traditional databases. If you "rummaged around" various sites on the Internet, looking for information on biotechnology, you'd come across a variety of information: for example, you'd probably locate university sponsored research papers, theses, company advertisements and promotional literature, discussion groups on the ethics of various biotechnology endeavors, government statistics on how well the U.S. industry is doing in the field an outlook on international competition, lists of consultants, names of research laboratories with current projects and names of scientists, news reports on trends in the industry and much more. Most of this information would not cost anything, since the majority of the information on the Internet is still free.

So, unlike a targeted database search, where you are often looking for formally published and structured information that will answer a specific question, searching the Internet is normally more appropriate when you are more open to accept whatever is there that you happen to come across.

There is, though, one area where the Internet really does shine for the business researcher: that is, for finding expert opinion as a way of getting answers to quick, close-ended questions. The next section examines why.

❏ FINDING EXPERT OPINION

If there's one area where the Internet lives up to its hype, it is in its capability to help you find experts and people who may know answers to your questions. The Internet's "culture" so to speak, is an information-sharing one. If you know something about a topic, and someone posts a question on it and you can help them, you do so.

The best place on the Internet to find experts who can answer questions is in one of the thousands of discussion groups (the list servs and usenet groups) where people with similar interests link up electronically to exchange ideas and debate current issues within the field. Again, as with everything on the Internet, the scope of these discussion groups runs the gamut. You'll find newsgroups discussing offbeat and arcane topics from alien sightings and left-handedness to traditional business related subjects like investment strategies and computer technology trends.

Once you have signed up with a list serv or joined a usenet group, you should just "hang around" for awhile, reading posted messages to get a feel for how the group operates, what some of the unwritten rules are, and what are some of the hot issues (reading messages without posting any yourself is known as "lurking" on the Internet). Then, when you feel fairly confident, you can add your own 2¢ to the discussion, or throw out a question to the group. Odds are, you will receive several responses and answers from the group—usually within 12-48 hours.

Typically, those responses will answer your question, and, other than thanking those group members who helped you, that will be the end of the matter. On occasion, though, you may find contradictory responses. For example, say you post a message in a listserv called online-news, where a few hundred people regularly discuss electronic newspapers, and you ask the group whether the *New York Times* is working on launching an electronic newspaper on the Internet. And, say you get back three responses: one person says, yes, the *New York Times* is on the Internet, and gives you an Internet address to find them; another says, no, but that they are working on it; and the third says that the *New York Times* can be found on America Online, but is not on the Internet.

If this occurs: where the answers are contradictory, there's usually no cause for concern: you can sit back and watch, as other members of the group, who've also seen this contradictory or confusing information, post their own messages to help clear up the confusion. Almost always, within another day or two, other members come to the rescue with additional information, and help sort it all out. On the Internet, things have a way of working themselves out, and significantly, it's done without anyone in charge.

So in this example, you might get postings from someone who, say, just read a press release from the *New York Times*, or someone who is researching the topic for a paper, or even from someone at the *New York Times* itself. (In this case, you'd find out that although the *New York Times* is indeed on America Online, it only contains a portion of the full paper, and that the current service on the Internet is just an 8 page fax summary. A full world wide web version of the paper is not due out for several more months. Each of the original postings, then, was correct, but each person only had a limited view of the situation. It took additional people to help round out the whole picture.)

And this is what is so different about the Internet, compared to traditional information sources and information vendors. It is a self-working, self-policing mechanism, completely decentralized, inherently egalitarian, and relies on the cooperation and self-interest of members to make it work.

For an information savvy businessperson, the Internet, then is another important, though nontraditional tool for gathering and absorbing information and knowledge. It has its potential drawbacks: you have few cues for knowing the credibility, background or knowledge of the person whose making a statement or offering you an answer to your question, (as illustrated by the now-famous New Yorker cartoon of a dog at a computer telling a nearby canine companion that "On the Internet, nobody knows you're a dog"), and you are never quite sure ahead of time what kind of response you are going to get to your inquiries. But the Internet can be an amazing short-cut to an answer, especially for very obscure matters, or when a traditional source cannot be located.

One of the best anecdotes illustrating the Internet's remarkable serendipitous nature was published a couple years ago in an issue of *Online* magazine. The authors, two business librarians, told of an incident where a colleague posted a message on an Internet discussion group saying that he had been unable to locate the source of a particular quote attributed to Albert Einstein, and was wondering if anyone could help him find it. A day or so later, a reply came back by the renowned physicist Marvin Minsky, who said that the quote came from a book he had written where he cited that remark by Einstein after hearing him make that remark in class!

It's just this kind of "wow" effect—finding unexpected and on-target responses that makes the Internet such a powerful and unusual tool for the information age.

Some examples of useful business sites

Although it is well beyond the scope of this book (and probably impossible for any book!) to provide anywhere near a comprehensive list of business information sites on the Internet, the appendix lists some of the best in order to give you a flavor of what you can find.

Interestingly, some of the best information found on the Internet is derived from the U.S. federal government, which has been making an effort to get a large amount of the most sought-after data available on the Internet. Some of the most broadly useful ones include the U.S. Bureau of the Census, Stat-USA which contains the National Trade Database, and EDGAR, which provides access to electronic filings from public companies around the U.S. For a further description, and contact information, see the Appendix.

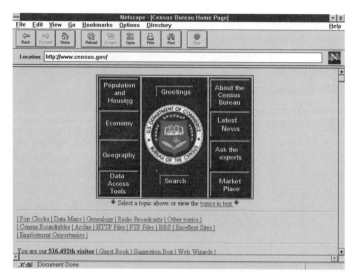

The Bureau of the Census is just one of many data-rich web sites available for free or low cost from the U.S. government. The Bureau of Census web address is: http//www.census.gov.

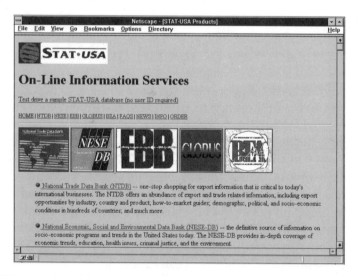

Stat-USA is produced by the U.S. Department of Commerce, and provides a wide variety of useful free and low cost business information, including access to the National Trade Data Bank, economic statistics, export assistance, and much more. Its address is: http:www.stat-usa.gov.

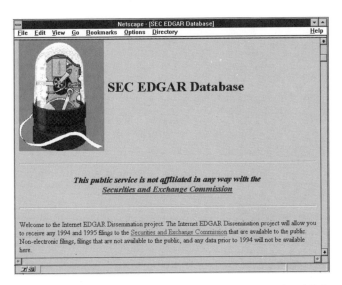

EDGAR is a free Internet site that provides access to thousands of U.S. public company document filings with the SEC. Its web address is: http// www.sec.gov/edgarhp.htm.

Although it is still not completely possible to do a comprehensive search across the entire Internet, during the last couple of years a variety of very good free and fee-based search software has been developed to help users find what they need. These very useful tools organize data on the Internet by indexing sites based on subject and by allowing users to perform some basic keyword searching. Some of these search tools are free, while others charge a small fee. The most popular of these include search tools called Alta Vista, Deja News, Yahoo, InfoSeek, Open Text, NlightN, and others. See Appendix 3 for the web addresses.

The screen shots on the following pages illustrate how these search engines work. On the first two screens, Yahoo helps us search the Internet for information on Alternative Medicine; On the second two screens, a sophisticated search engine called Open Text helps us to find information on sports marketing; On the third set of screens, we search for sites on the biotechnology industry, using Digital's Alta Vista search engine.

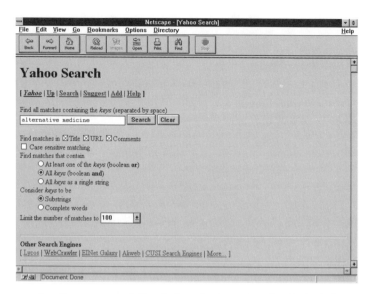

Yahoo searches its own preexisting index of categories of web site information as well as the text of the sites themselves to locate a match.

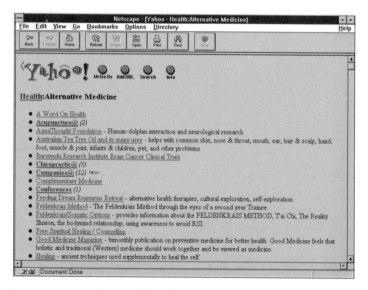

Here Yahoo returns a listing of the sites it has indexed under its category of "alternative medicine."

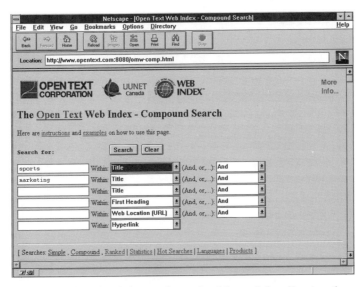

Open Text allows for a sophisticated search of the web by allowing the user to specify what portion of the web site the keywords must appear, and permits creating a longer, complex search.

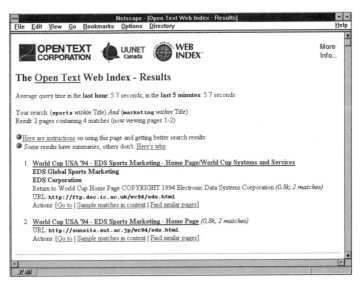

Open Text here displays a list of web sites, along with the hot links, to those that contained the words "sports" and "marketing" in the title.

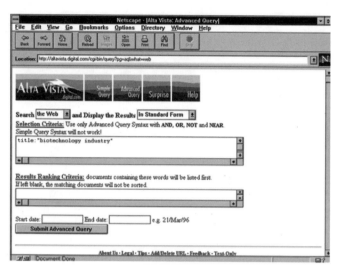

Alta Vista, a search engine introduced by Digital Equipment Co. in February, 1996, is fast and powerful. Here we search for web pages with the phrase "biotechnology industry" in its title.

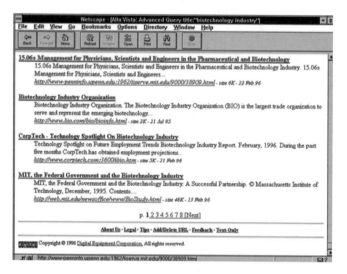

Alta Vista found 73 web pages with the phrase "biotechnology industry" in its title. It displays a list of the first ten. Let's look in more detail at the CorpTech document.

```
┌─────────────────────────────────────────────────────────────────────┐
│   Netscape - [CorpTech - Technology Spotlight On Biotechnology Industry]   ▼│◊│
│ File  Edit  View  Go  Bookmarks  Options  Directory  Window  Help         │
├─────────────────────────────────────────────────────────────────────┤
│  Technology Spotlight on Future Employment Trends                         │
│  Biotechnology Industry Report                                            │
│                                                                           │
│  March, 1996                                                              │
│  ─────────────────────────────────────────────────────────────           │
│                                                                           │
│  During the past five months CorpTech has obtained employment projections from 122 of the 684 technology companies │
│  involved in biotechnology, with under 1,000 employees listed in the CorpTech Directory. Over 25% of the surveyed  │
│  companies plan to expand their work force during the next year by an average of 12.3%, creating 388 new jobs and generating │
│  sales opportunities for their suppliers. More than one company in nine projects growth of over 25%.              │
│                                                                           │
│  The 122 surveyed biotechnology companies expected to increase their combined total employment by an average of 4.3%, │
│  from 9,019 now to 9,407 next year. Over 2% of America's 31,060 small and mid-sized high-tech manufacturers are now │
│  active in this technology, with 44,912 employees.                        │
└─────────────────────────────────────────────────────────────────────┘
```

	# of Comp	Employ Now	Proj	Chng	Chg %
Growing at over 25%	14	344	160	46.5 %	
Growing at under 25%	17	2,816	228	8.1 %	
Stable employment	91	5,859	0	-	
Shrinking companies	0	0	0	.0 %	
	-----	-------	------	-----	
Survey totals	122	9,019	388	4.3 %	
March, 1995 survey	137	12,561	672	5.3 %	

On this site, CorpTech, a leading researcher and publisher on high technology companies, provides statistics on employment trends in the biotechnology industry.

Finding what you want

The fact that the Internet is a global, self-regulating, decentralized information network is a double-edged sword. On the positive side, it makes the net a fun, exciting, and rarely boring place to be and to explore. But it can also make it maddeningly frustrating to find out whether a specific piece of information is on the net, and if it is, where to locate it. Sure, it's fun to browse around the net, hoping to land on some nugget of valuable information that is going to help you in your business or your personal life. But browsing around takes a lot of time. Online expert Peter Jåcso has called the process "rummaging around a hypergarage sale." Great if you've got hours of time on your hands, but who in business has 20 minutes of free time, let alone hours?

Magazines and Newspapers

A fast growing segment of the Internet are electronic journals and newspapers. Some are simply equivalents to the already existing print copy journals (e.g. ranging from popular ones like *Time*, *The Atlantic*, etc. to more technical and scientific journals) while others were actually begun online and are available only in electronic format.

The jury is still out as to how successful online magazines and newspapers will be. While electronic media offers the advantages of instant searchability, instant delivery, and timeliness, there are also significant disadvantages. It is more difficult to browse through online media, most people still prefer the feel and flexibility of paper, and do not enjoy reading long screenloads of text on a computer.

So far, it appears that electronic versions of magazines and newspapers are most successful for very targeted purposes, such as searching directory listings (e.g. classifieds, reviews, phone books, events, etc.), for a quick take on headline news, or for those readers who enjoy the interactive abilities of the medium, and like discussing the articles and related issues with other readers as well as the writers and editors of the journal.

However, it is really too early to predict where these electronic journals are heading. One popular site by Time-Warner Inc., called Pathfinder, features articles and editorials from many popular national magazines (the web address is http:// www.pathfinder.com)

One area, though, where electronic journals are already seen as a legitimate addition to print is, not surprisingly, the computer industry. And within the computer field, not surprisingly, the most popular segment are those that have anything to do with online and the Internet. (After all, where would there be a better place for such a publication to find its readers?)

There are some success stories, though. One of the most popular and acclaimed of the new electronic journals is *Wired* magazine's world wide web site, called HotWired. Unlike most other media that have just launched an electronic version of their already existing print journal, the staff at HotWired looked at the Internet medium fresh, and created its electronic information product so as to take advantage of the medium's unique possibilities. HotWired is colorful, playful, extremely interactive, and the writing is lively and iconoclastic. As of late 1995, the site was free, although users need to register. (You can connect to HotWired at: http//:www.hotwired.com. and check it out yourself.)

But unless you are researching the computer or online field, you probably don't need to be too concerned about using electronic journals as a research tool on the Internet (at least for now). The best way to tap into emerging knowledge via the Internet remains the discussion groups, as described above.

As discussed earlier in this book, a special type of new media are the "customized electronic news" delivery vendors, which will deliver to your PC, on a daily basis, your own personalized newspaper, based on your own interests and information needs. While some of these vendors make their services available on the Internet (such as Individual Inc.'s NewsPage on the world wide web: [http://www.newspage.com]), these services can be delivered a variety of ways, such as by fax, your own firm's network, satellite, and so on, and they are not limited to the Internet.

Where's all this Leading?

Although predicting where the Internet is leading (and leading all of us) is about as exact a procedure as trying to pin down the future of the world economy or the planet's weather, let's give it our best shot.

An easy prediction is that Internet access will get faster and that bandwidth (the size of the "pipeline" that the data travels through between computers) will increase. What this means is that you will be able to download more information and more elaborate multimedia, such as full video, much faster than is possible now.

There may also be some type of technological convergence of all the separate databases and systems. That is, the online databases, the entire Internet, CD-ROMs, consumer online services, and all the digitized print material—as well as some video materials—will all be accessible from the same platform. And, there will be a standardized method for searching and accessing the information across all these formats and media. There are already some efforts being made along these lines. But progress, in our view, will be slower than some have predicted, and time will tell whether this state of information nirvana will prove to be doable or an impossible dream. For the near-term future to the year 2000, it's more likely that most access to the Internet will be via PC and modem, with increasing speeds.

We believe that you can also expect to see an explosion of "home made" world wide web pages over the Internet, which will have enormous implications relating to information dissemination. Internet service providers and consumer online services such as America Online, Prodigy, etc., in late 1995 began offering their users templates for designing their own world wide web pages for dissemination to the millions of Internet users around the globe. We believe this will have dramatic ramifications, as it represents the end of the traditional technical and economic barriers of entry to becoming an information provider: that is, the need for a printing press and a physical distribution mechanism such as a fleet of delivery trucks. The world wide web demolishes those barriers to mass publishing. The job of ferreting out the valuable business data from the trivia and junk-information, then, will likely become even more difficult.

This explosion of information on the Internet will spur development of even more sophisticated and powerful search engines and tools to make navigation and Internet research simpler. The most advanced of these are called "Intelligent Agents." These are software products that you program to automatically and "behind the scenes" search the Internet to seek out, retrieve and deliver to you just the kind of information that fits your needs. Still, it remains to be seen whether better search tools and intelligent agents will truly be able to tame the Internet.

From an even broader perspective, the growing millions of people connected over the Internet discussing issues, sharing information, and finding communities of common interest represents a quantum leap in the human ability to exchange information and communicate. By transcending both physical space and time limitations, the Internet vastly increases people's ability to link minds to create new knowledge. For the information savvy businessperson, this could mean an exponential advance in instantly locating the best expertise on a topic from around the globe, and then leveraging that knowledge as a strategic advantage.

According to some, the Internet is even moving the entire species forward in a new evolutionary leap. And there are those who dismiss the Internet as just the latest version of CB-Radio: a fad that will pass.

Our view is that, while we don't feel qualified to speak of the Internet's evolutionary role for our species, we do not dismiss it as another CB-Radio fad. There are already too many people on the Internet, too much invested in making it happen, and too many inherent benefits to instantaneous, cheap worldwide communication and publishing. The Internet is here, it is powerful, and it is changing how we communicate.

Our real concerns though, for the businessperson, are more practical:

• Although it is true that more and more information is becoming available online, the great bulk of the world's knowledge can still only be found in print. Most of the popular consumer magazines, social science literature, and a good deal of scientific and technical data is not available in any form online. This is also true for newspapers—particularly for those published outside the U.S. You can never assume that if it's not online then it doesn't exist. It will be many years, if ever, that we reach the state that all the world's knowledge is digitized and made available over electronic networks.

• As data on the Internet continues to proliferate, remember that data alone is not information; and that information alone is not knowledge. Data must be organized to become information; and information must be put into a context to become knowledge: and that's the resource you need to succeed in business. You will still need to supply the context (e.g. what does this information mean to your industry, your product, your strategic plans) to transform all kinds of data—whether it's from a hyper-linked Internet web site or the Almanac on your bookshelf—to become knowledge.

• Finally, remember too that while speed—currency of data, rate of transmission, or how quickly you can get access—has become of enormous value and importance to business, it still takes time to organize what you've uncovered, to put it into that context, and to reflect on its greater significance. Speed is a key means to your end. But it is not the end itself, and can defeat your end if it means you're not taking enough time just to sit and think.

The end, in business, is to be competitive: the Internet can help you get there. But you must still supply the wisdom, to turn data and information into knowledge and action.

9

A Prescription for Information Paralysis

A peculiar disease afflicts all kinds of people in America. It attacks executives, professionals, and even homemakers with equal impunity. The best doctors rarely diagnose it, certainly cannot cure it, and, in fact, are often afflicted with it themselves.

It's called "information paralysis."

Information paralysis is the inability to proceed from a question to the actual act of beginning to gather the information needed for the answer. Otherwise intelligent people who understand the value of information and have even gone so far as to formulate extremely perceptive questions can do nothing further. Total paralysis strikes. They don't know what to do, where to start, or how to go about it. Fear takes over.

The best cure for information paralysis is to become an expert information specialist who is thoroughly familiar with thousands of sources of information. This book is not designed to help you do that. For that matter, we suspect that you do not want to abandon your present career. Instead, we'll try to provide the second-best cure which is offering the information and advice contained right here in this chapter.

The good news is that even as the number and types of information continues to grow, it does not have to be out of your control.

There are, we believe, three major strategies you can pursue that will help you not only deal with what author Saul Wurman calls "information anxiety" but assist you in actually learning how to use and leverage the power of the information explosion to make you and your business more effective, powerful and competitive.

The first strategy is what most of this book is devoted to: becoming information savvy, knowing the "stuff" of information. This means, understanding the different kinds of information that exist, knowing where to look to find what you need, being able to distinguish high quality data from bad data, and being aware of the different ways and outlets that information is disseminated. This will give you the grounding, the "knowledge about knowledge" that you must have to effectively work with, mold, and direct this powerful beast. You need to understand information in order to make it work for you. The bulk of this chapter is devoted to giving you a basic understanding of the types of information that exist and an understanding of the basic categories most information needs fall into.

The second strategy is organizational and managerial. It means taking the time to figure out what your three to five or so most important business challenges and priorities are for the next year or two years, and then making sure that the time that you spend digesting information relates to those priorities. (This implies, of course, knowing the top priorities [i.e. objectives and goals] of your organization, your own department, and your own role within your department. By doing this you also put the "context" back into information that has become increasingly decontextualized.)

The third strategy is psychological. Because the pace of technological change exceeds our capability to adjust and deal with it —what Toffler perceived as the emerging "Future Shock" all the way back in 1970 (if only we had the technological challenges of that era!), you must actively confront how you view the information explosion, and work to reorient your beliefs so that they work for you, and not against you.

The way you react to the information age can be viewed as the result of two distinct phenomena: 1) the external givens, those elements that you cannot change, and 2) how you perceive those externals, which is under your control. We'll concentrate here on number two.

Say you take the following view of the information explosion: "there's just too much to deal with...I'll never get to all this stuff...I can't get anything important done...and...THIS IS ALL JUST DRIVING ME CRAZY!" And, sure, that would be your reality, since you feel out of control, as a result of your own, self-created expectations, demands, and beliefs.

But this is unnecessary. The two insights that you need to think about carefully and remember to apply are:

1. there are healthy and productive ways to view a situation and there are unhealthy, nonproductive ways.

2. you have the power to choose how you view a situation.*

So, instead of holding self-defeating beliefs as expressed above, you can choose, if you desire, to replace them with another view that is just as "legitimate", but one that is more productive and realistic: For example, instead of those above self-defeating beliefs you could choose to tell yourself, this instead: There is a lot to deal with...I won't get to all of it, I'll just have to try to get to the most important items...It won't be possible for me to get everything I want done, but that's business life in the 1990s...dealing with all this information can be a pain in the neck, but I'll survive.

You can take some control of the information explosion and reduce, if not eliminate your information paralysis. In summary, this means: 1) understanding the types of information sources that exist and how they are organized; 2) defining your business priorities and concentrating on utilizing information that will

* Albert Ellis has written extensively on human ability to substitute rational and healthy beliefs for irrational and destructive ones. See, among others, his book: A New Guide to Rational Living, (Wilshire, 1975)

forward just those goals; 3) changing the way you view living in the information age.

Tom Peters has said "Everyone knows that leveraging knowledge is central to tomorrow's success. But they miss 95% of the equation. It's 5% technology (like networked data, group-ware and the like) and 95% psychology. "

Now let's get back to strategy number one, and provide you with a full examination of the types of information sources that exist, and how they are organized:

There are really only four basic types of sources of information: government sources; associations; commercial publishers, services, and sources; and libraries and educational institutions.

Note that another type of information source, electronic information over databases and the Internet, are not covered in this chapter, since they were covered in detail in Chapters 7 and 8.

Government Sources

Governmental agencies are a tremendous source of all types of information. This includes federal, state, and local governments.

❏ FEDERAL GOVERNMENT

The United States government is one of the biggest information-providers in the world. The various divisions and agencies of the Federal Government produce countless books, periodicals, pamphlets, and data sources every year. Topics run the gamut from helpful consumer "how-to" pamphlets to technical scientific briefings to business start-up guides to international political analyses. It would be impossible to describe even in a whole book all of the different information resources published by the Federal Government.

Each major department of the Federal Government contains scores of subagencies and bureaus, each with its own publications and areas of specialization. For example, one of the best sources of business information, the United States Department of Commerce, consists of these smaller agencies and bureaus:

- Bureau of the Census.
- Bureau of Economic Analysis.
- International Trade Administration.
- Minority Business Development Agency.
- National Bureau of Standards.
- National Oceanic and Atmospheric Administration.
- National Technical Information Service.
- Patent and Trademark Office.

Each of these divisions has its own information collection and dissemination operations. This pattern is repeated in most of the other government agencies, e.g., the departments of agriculture, defense, and energy, and bodies like the Securities and Exchange Commission, the Federal Communications Commission, the Food and Drug Administration, and the Environmental Protection Agency.

Many of these agencies, in addition to collecting and disseminating information, also operate full-scale information clearinghouses, such as the National Center for Health Statistics (in the Department of Health and Human Services) or the Office of Educational Research and Improvement (in the Department of Education).

There is a monumental amount of published information emanating from the Federal Government, everything from basic reference books like the *Statistical Abstract of the United States*, published by the Bureau of the Census, to obscure technical manuals on scientific discoveries from federal laboratories. There are basic sources like *County Business Patterns*, which contains statistics on county, state, and overall United States employment, size of reporting business units, and payrolls for fifteen broad industry categories; and *Survey of Current Business*, which is the official source for the Gross National Product figure, among other key statistics. But much of the government's data resources are unpublished as well.

For example, there are countless immigration records—but these are not published in a formal sense; you would have to request them if you wanted them. And some federal information sources do not even exist in printed form. For instance, there are hundreds of expert analysts who work in the Department of State who specialize in studying and analyzing different countries. They do not publish their findings, but can be telephoned and queried by people who have relevant questions.

Another federal information source is the United States Congress. Both the Senate and the House have committees and subcommittees (not to mention task forces and project teams) that collect loads of information, much of which gets published in one form or another. Much of this information is provided by expert witnesses who testify at congressional hearings. For example, if you wanted some inside facts on the 900-phone number industry, a recent hearing on data privacy called on a variety of expert witnesses who provided key insights into the marketing of the telecommunications industry. (For information on how to access this data, see the appendices.)

Another federal source is the court system, which includes the federal and state courts, as well as special courts such as the United States Customs Court, the United States Tax Court, and the United States Court of Claims.

During the last few years the federal government has been making a major effort to convert a large number of its print information sources to electronic format. Today you can access a good deal of some of the most widely useful government information such as census data and business statistical series on CD-ROM and over the Internet. Many libraries offer free access to government CD-ROMs for its patrons.

❑ STATE GOVERNMENT

A great deal of useful business information is available from the states. In fact, in recent years, as the Federal Government has shrunk and cut back services, many of the federal agencies' duties and responsibilities have been picked up by the State governments. Consequently, they now collect and disseminate more information.

Each state differs in the precise types of information it makes available, but there are certain similarities. For example, you can normally find a "secretary of state" office that contains a number of records about companies incorporated in that state. An "economic development" (or similarly named) office may have information and statistics about general economic conditions in the state, as would a "licensing bureau" that issues permits for various regulated businesses, such as real estate brokers or pharmacists. One very useful office is that of the "state attorney general," which keeps records on any criminal investigations against companies operating within the state.

Here is a list of the typical types of offices you will find in a State government:

- Aging
- Agriculture
- Air Pollution
- Alcohol and Drug Abuse
- Arts
- Banking
- Civil Rights
- Consumer Affairs
- Criminal Justice
- Disabled Citizens
- Disaster Preparedness
- Education
- Energy
- Environment
- Fish and Game
- Hazardous Materials
- Health
- Highways
- Housing
- Labor
- Mental Health
- Natural Resources
- Taxation
- Tourism
- Transportation
- Women

Most states also produce what are known as "state industrial directories," which are valuable listings of manufacturing and other types of companies operating within the state.

❑ LOCAL GOVERNMENTS

Finally, a variety of useful information can be found in county, city, and town offices. For example, county and city clerks keep a wealth of data on births, deaths, marriages, and divorces. They also keep records on property holdings and permits. Specific departments also keep other kinds of records. For example, most localities have a "buildings" division that issues permits for businesses that want to put up a new building. All of these records are normally available for the asking.

This brings us to our next point: how much of this governmental data is available to the public? *The vast majority of records and information collected by the different governmental agencies is available to any individual or business for the asking.* The Freedom of Information Act of 1966 requires federal agencies to provide the public with any identifiable records upon request, unless the information falls into a special exempted category such as national defense or personal data. If you are having trouble obtaining some information you think you legitimately should have, you should file a formal Freedom of Information request (which can be appealed if you are turned down), or contact the Freedom of Information Clearinghouse in Washington, DC, for further assistance.

Associations

A fantastic source for all kinds of information is associations. Today there are tens of thousands of organizations around the country devoted to thousands of different subjects. Types of associations range from the well-known professional ones, like the American Medical Association and the American Booksellers Association, to lesser-known industry organizations like the International Academy of Twirling Teachers and the National Association for Veterinarian Acupuncture, to special-interest business groups like the Valve Manufacturers Association or the World Insulation and Acoustic Congress.

A casual thumbing through the "bible" of associations, Gale Research's *Encyclopedia of Associations*, which lists over 22,000 associations, reveals the incredible scope of these groups. Want to know about the skies? Try the International Society of Planetariums, which has hundreds of members. Thinking of getting into raising sheep? Depending on what breed of sheep captures your fancy, you can call any one of the more than 30 different sheep breeder associations. Got a new-age cure for an old ailment? You might want to check with the American Holistic Medical Association.

Associations are great starting points when you're looking for information. Frequently, they have their own libraries and publish statistics and other facts on the industries or activities they represent. Furthermore, they are usually quite cooperative in answering questions because, after all, they exist to promote the interest of their members. Of course, you should keep in mind that their information is not necessarily the most objective.

Commercial Publishers, Services, and Sources

There is an absolute multitude of books, periodicals, directories, indices, guides, statistical compilations, services, and sources that are commercially produced for informational purposes.

❏ REFERENCE PUBLICATIONS

Included in this category are such standard company directories as *Dun & Bradstreet Million Dollar Directory, Standard & Poor's Register*, and *Ward's Business Directory*, all of which provide facts and statistics on larger businesses; indices like *Business Periodicals Index* and *Funk & Scott*, which identify business periodical articles on companies, industries, products, etc.; and countless other guides and statistical compilations.

In fact, there are so many reference guides and directories that there is even a "directory of directories"—*Directories in Print*, published by Gale Research. This guide is actually one of the best places to begin a literature search on a topic, as it covers so many subjects and is so easy to find and use.

❑ PERIODICALS

Just as there is an association for virtually any conceivable topic, so too is there a publication on just about anything, for just about anyone. For example, if you are interested in alternatives to chemicals, you could get a copy of the *Journal of Pesticide Reform*; or if your fancy is flying rodents, there is the *Bat Research News*. Other publications you might browse through include *Diesel Fuel Oils Magazine* or *Hosiery & Underwear*.

Should you want to find a specific magazine or newsletter, there are a few different directories of periodicals you can check. Two of the best-known are the *Gale Directory of Publications and Broadcast Media* and the *Standard Periodical Directory*. Both are available at most libraries, and both list thousands of special-interest publications.

One other useful aspect of trade publications is that many of them publish special issues that can be valuable information sources. For example, some publish annual "buyer's guide" issues that list names and addresses of manufacturers and products. Other special issues include annual statistical compilations, such as salary surveys or year-end sales statistics. Because these publications are usually supported by advertising, they are generally very inexpensive.

❑ SPECIAL INFORMATION SERVICES

Depending upon the industry or profession and its information needs, there are a host of special services. For example, R.L. Polk & Company and Ward's Reports, Inc. both publish a variety of data on the automotive industry. There are loose-leaf services that will keep you updated weekly, monthly, or even daily in a field of interest. Organizations like the Conference Board and the Research Institute of America (both in New York City) publish a variety of reports on business management, affairs, and other topics. Firms like Arthur D. Little and the Gartner Group produce special reports on industries and markets; these are mailed periodically to members, who pay large annual fees and can call upon the firms for consultation. One of the most well-known information services is Dun & Bradstreet, which, along with its many other activities, issues credit reports that are among the few in-depth sources of information available about privately held companies.

❏ INVESTIGATIVE SERVICES

If you are about to sign a million-dollar deal with someone you met only a few months ago, you obviously need to know with as much certainty as possible the background, credentials, and integrity of that person. But background information on individual executives, information on privately held companies, and other types of information, such as litigation histories, are extremely difficult to obtain. While much of this type of data *is* available in public records and databases if you look hard and long enough, sometimes you may need the service of an expert investigator. There are a number of investigative services throughout the country that do investigative reports on corporations and executives. Among the best known are companies like Bishop's Services Inc. and Kroll Associates in New York City, the Dow Services Group in Boston, and Beltrante & Associates in Washington, DC.

❏ ONLINE DATABASES AND THE INTERNET

As mentioned at the beginning of this chapter, online databases and the Internet are covered in detail in Chapters 7 and 8. You should note, however, that many commercial databases and Internet sources are also available in print, CD-ROM, and other formats. For example, the *F&S Index of Corporations and Industries* (published by Predicasts) is an index that covers company, industry, and product information from thousands of periodicals. It was originally available only in printed form, but is now also an online database.

❏ MARKET RESEARCH AND SURVEY FIRMS

Market research and survey firms are engaged mostly in primary research activities of one sort or another—i.e., they interview people to find out their opinions, preferences, behaviors, and the like. Or they may directly measure, via surveys, things like sales of a particular product or size of an industry. There are three major types of survey techniques:

1. *Consumer Panels.* These are carefully selected groups of individual consumers who periodically report on various aspects of their buying behavior, attitudes, and intentions. National Family Opinion, Inc., is a well-known firm that runs consumer panels. These panels are highly useful when you want, for example, to have a continual measurement of consumer attitudes toward your product.

2. *Syndicated Audits.* In syndicated audits, firms like A.C. Nielsen Company continuously monitor the movement of products through stores by type of product, brand, and even package size. They compile the results and sell them for very high prices. UPC bar-code scanning has added a great new level of detail to the information being captured by these firms, and has made their services even more valuable.

3. *Published Field Interviews.* Typical of this type of firm is the F.W. Dodge Division of McGraw-Hill Information Systems. It collects construction data through hundreds of interviews, supplementing this with other information and publishing thousands of reports each month on building projects.

4. *Consumer Surveys.* Consumer survey firms conduct surveys on either a syndicated or custom basis. Typical of syndicated surveys are the regularly-issued Gallup polls, where the results are offered to many participants. Some firms run what

are called "omnibus" surveys, which regularly survey a national probability sample of respondents. Custom surveys, of course, can be done on just about any subject.

Libraries and Educational Institutions

Libraries are, of course, fabulous sources. It is important, though, to distinguish between the various types of libraries. Types of libraries are public, university, and "special" libraries.

The best public libraries are normally those located in larger cities, as these have the most complete reference collections, as well as access to the latest computer-based retrieval technologies. Many libraries make available to their patrons state-of-the-art CD-ROM data retrieval systems that can be used to obtain abstracts of articles published in hundreds of business periodicals, cutting research time significantly. Some of the most popular of these systems are produced by a company called the Information Access Company.

University and college libraries are also excellent resource centers. You will often find that a college or university library offers resources superior to those of a large public library. (This is because public libraries are often strapped for cash, while college libraries are often privately funded.) Many college and university libraries will allow anyone to come in and use their resources, although you won't be allowed to check anything out.

Special libraries are located in businesses or other institutions, such as museums, research institutes, and so forth. While they are not "public" in that they are not funded by tax dollars, many of them allow outside researchers to come in and use their information resources. So, for example, if you were researching the lighting industry, you might try and see if you could use General Electric's corporate library, or that of another firm in the industry.

Often overlooked—but potentially valuable—sources of information are educational institutions and publications.

Individual college and university professors are information resources in their areas of expertise, and many universities have set up "faculty databases" that offer specialized professorial knowledge online. Doctoral dissertations can be excellent sources for research on obscure or narrow subjects not covered elsewhere. A computerized compilation of all dissertations can be searched by contacting University Microfilms of Ann Arbor, Michigan.

Related organizations with educational missions can also be worthwhile sources. For example, most museums have a library or information services department—the Smithsonian Institution in Washington, DC, is a treasure-house of free data. There are directories of non-profit research centers, too: you can check Gale Research's *Research Centers Directory* to find the names of—and contacts for—thousands of different university, government, and non-profit research organizations.

Some Sources of Sources

What we have done so far in this chapter is to give you a feel for some of the major types of sources that you can turn to when you have a question you need answered. We have given you starting points so that you won't be afflicted with information paralysis. Whatever your question, an answer can most likely be found within information stored or disseminated by a government body, an association or group, a library, or a commercial publisher, service, or database.

But which government body? Which service?

For specific listings, you'll need to check a complete source book, the names of which are listed in Appendix I. But if you don't want to read a source book, there is some "quick" assistance available. You can check one of the "sources of sources" guides. These guides are so all-encompassing and so valuable that we will list them here.

What Federal Government body or agency can help me?

Who Knows: A Guide to Washington Experts
Washington Researchers
PO Box 19005
Washington, DC 20036

Is there an association that can help?

The Encyclopedia of Associations
Gale Research Company
835 Penobscott Building
Detroit, MI 48226

Is there a sourcebook or directory that can help me?

Directories in Print
Gale Research Company
835 Penobscott Building
Detroit, MI 48226

Is there an information finding firm that can help me?

Burwell's World Directory of Information Brokers
Burwell Enterprises
3724 FM 1960 West
Suite 214
Houston, TX 77068

Is there a database that can answer my question?

Gale's Directory of Online Databases
Gale Research Company
835 Penobscot Building
Detroit, MI 48226

Is there a periodical on this subject?

The Standard Periodical Directory
Oxbridge Communications
150 Fifth Avenue
Suite 236
New York, NY 10011

Is there a magazine or journal covering this subject?

Gale Directory of Publications and Broadcast Media
Gale Research Company
835 Penobscott Building
Detroit, MI 48226

Is there a market research firm or published study that can help me?

International Directory of Marketing
Research Houses and Services
American Marketing Association
135 West 50th Street
New York, NY 10020

Findex: The Directory of Market Research Reports,
Studies, and Surveys
Cambridge Information Group
7200 Wisconsin Avenue
Bethesda, MD 20814

Is there a library that can help me?

Directory of Special Libraries and Information Centers
Gale Research Company
835 Penobscott Building
Detroit, MI 48226

American Library Directory
R.R. Bowker/Reed Reference Publishing
121 Chanlon Road
New Providence, NJ 07974

Categories of Information

The second part of our cure for information paralysis is to help you gain an understanding of the different categories of external information.

If you are in business or in a profession, there are certain categories of information that you are likely to need. Indeed, it is inconceivable that you can exist properly without them.

First of all, you need information about your competition—about other companies, organizations, or individuals. You must have information both about individual competitors and about your industry or profession as a whole.

Secondly, you need information about your market, whether it consists of individual consumers or of other organizations and companies.

You need information about the world around you, insofar as it may affect your business or profession. This means that you need to be kept up to date on politics, economics, culture, government, and the environment.

You need to know the best ways to do business. This means you need information on how to manage, organize, and run your business.

You need information on scientific and technological developments. If you're not "in" on the latest, you could be "down and out" shortly.

Finally, you need information on laws, regulations, and other restrictions that may affect the way you do business.

If you can start thinking in terms of categories, you can begin to break down your information needs so that you can properly direct yourself to the right types of sources.

Know Your Competition

In a country as populated as ours, you have competition—whatever field you are in. And most assuredly your success will depend, to some degree, on the amount and quality of information you can glean about your competitors. Whether you are a consultant, or you are running a small hair salon, or you are the president of a multinational corporation, information about your competition is not an elective. Yet the number of people who ignore this is astounding.

Multitudes of executives and professionals lose their jobs and clients daily. Why is this so? Undoubtedly, it is because they are not performing their functions adequately. One of the keys to performance is having information about your competition. If you are not worried about your competition, chances are that you will lose your job; and if you are self-employed, you will probably lose your business.

What kind of information should you have about your competition? You should know about their:

- Management structure.
- Product lines.
- Sales.
- Financial condition.
- Facilities.
- New products.
- New directions and developments.
- Marketing approaches.

Is this kind of information available? In all likelihood, much of it is. How do you get it? The means vary.

One approach is word of mouth. An old funny story illustrates this: Dave and Sam were partners in the ladies' garment business for many years. During one season, they had incredibly bad luck. When they produced satins, organdies were the rage. When they produced nylon, cotton came into vogue. One day Dave came to work so depressed that he bid Sam goodbye and jumped out of their thirty-sixth-floor window. Sam ran to the open window, appalled. As Dave hurtled past the fourteenth floor, he looked into the window of their competitor and yelled up to his partner, "Sam, they're cutting velvets in there!" This is an extreme example of investigating your competition's "new products in development."

Word of mouth, however, is not always possible, nor is it always reliable. But if you start thinking about the different types of sources we described earlier, you can quickly begin to get a grasp of how to proceed.

For example, if your competitor is a publicly held corporation, then it must file information with the government. If that is so, then there must be an agency within the government that compiles or makes available such information. Of course, there is. It's the Securities and Exchange Commission

If your competitor is a privately held corporation, then it is likely that information about it will be much harder to find. But there are services like Dun & Bradstreet that will provide credit reports; there are published indices that might index anything that has been written about the company; there are local chambers of commerce that might keep data on how the company does business; there are investigative services that will look into the background of the company's principals; and so on.

Similarly, each of the types of sources we covered earlier probably has one or more items of data that can help you put together a complete picture of your competition.

But the primary reason for the necessity and urgency of finding information about your competition has undoubtedly occurred to you by now, and that is that all of these information-gathering methods are available to your competition as well! If you have competition, it is probably studying you at this very moment.

Know Your Market

All businesses need information on their markets. If you sell your product or service to individual consumers, then you are likely to need information about their habits, their buying patterns, their feelings, and their intentions. In that case, you would direct yourself toward the market research and survey firms that specialize in such things. Or you may want information about the products and services—competitive or related—that such consumers buy. In that case you may direct yourself to syndicated audits, which measure the movement of goods through retail outlets.

If you sell your product or service to businesses or organizations, then, in order to obtain information about your market, you'll have to get information on the industries you serve. You would direct yourself, therefore, to associations and trade periodicals that serve those industries. You might explore what the government knows about them.

Here's a tip on getting information about markets. When you need a quick look at the size of a market, try catalogs of mailing list firms. They are usually free and make for fascinating reading, not to mention the fact that they contain tremendous stores of marketing information. For example, let's assume you've just invented a revolutionary method for the disposal of toxic wastes. You figure it would sell to any company whose manufacturing produces toxins. But how many of them are there? Well, a glance at a mailing list catalog from a firm like Information Marketing Services Inc. in Vienna, Virginia, whose lists are available for rental, would show that there are 30,000 toxic waste generators. Of course, these types of lists may not include *all* of your potential market. But they do include a very important part of it—the part that can be reached by mail.

Another thing to keep in mind is that, generally speaking, the narrower the market, the more unlikely it is that data on it has been collected in a readily available format. The broader the market, the more available the data. Cosmetics would be a broad market; green eye shadow would be a narrow one. It is extremely easy to find studies that have already been published on the cosmetics industry and market. We know of no available complete study on green eye shadow, however.

The World

Every day, every section of your local newspaper has something in it that directly or indirectly affects your business or profession—including the advertisements. The newspaper may not give you a totally realistic picture of what the world is like (you must rely on your best judgment for that), but it does give you an accurate picture of how your community is perceiving the world, and, therefore, how its attitudes and values are being shaped and formed. You need this knowledge desperately for your own success in your business.

Moving further outward, national and international magazines and newspapers can give you both in-depth information and a wider perspective. If your business is to grow, you cannot afford to be provincial in your outlook.

All of these sources inform us about various aspects of the world. Unfortunately, we often need more information about the world than we realize. Fortunately, there are more sources than we can imagine.

Remember the example involving Vietnam in the database section of this book? To illustrate how you might suddenly need to be informed about countries far away, assume that you made the deal with the man in Vietnam and that you are now an exporter to that country. What's happening in Vietnam is now of paramount importance to you. You might now consult the *Nexis* database every month for updates on articles written about Vietnam. You'll want to consult the United States Federal Government expert on Vietnam. You'll want to know whether there are any private information services that can help. You'll discover a company called The Economist Intelligence Unit (previously called Business International and located in New York City) that specializes in collecting and disseminating information on business activity and economic developments in foreign countries. A new world of information sources and possibilities has opened up for you.

Evaluate Your Management Practices

We have a tendency to do things without considering whether we are doing them right or wrong, whether there is a better way, or how others are doing the same things.

Suppose you are an executive wanting to start a pension plan for your employees. Your first impulse might be to call in a pension expert. But you should think first about reading something on the subject. Why don't you? Lazy? Not necessarily. The answer comes back again to the lack of information consciousness. It is always fine to call in experts, but you yourself should be prepared for meeting with them.

Let's take another example. Suppose you wish to hire a computer systems manager. Yours is a small company that is growing quickly. You have a mini-computer and network, and you need someone to run it. How much must you pay a competent systems person? You might call a personnel agency and inquire. But the agency's answer is necessarily biased, isn't it? If you were an information-conscious person, you would immediately realize that there must be a regional salary survey of systems managers available, and that you could buy that survey.

The same holds true for expenditure norms like advertising, rent, and payroll. Some folks are afraid to discover that they have been managing their businesses or professions poorly for a very long time. But those people lack curiosity and have either discarded this book chapters ago or never purchased it at all.

Government Regulations

Government regulations on any level—town, country, state, or federal—are such an integral part of everyone's business or professional life that ignorance of this informational area can lead to total failure. Regulations are a vital part of your external business environment.

If, for example, you want to manufacture a new detergent and aren't aware that county regulations would automatically ban its production because of one of its chemical ingredients, you are courting disaster.

The one saving grace about this kind of information is that the government distributes published regulations free of charge on request. Your tax dollars pay for its dissemination. But you must take the time to send for it.

You now have the prescription for curing whatever degree

of information paralysis you are suffering from. But as with all prescriptions, two more steps are required: you must fill it and then use it. The types and sources of information are all there on the "medicinal" shelves. You have only to reach for them, according to your particular needs.

10

Creating Your Own Information-Finding System

We stated at the beginning of the book that most people have little idea how to find out what they need to know. Given this, it is not surprising that most people—and the organizations they work in—do not have an effective information-finding system. How to create one is the subject of this chapter.

Effective information-finding systems begin with the individual—with you.

Let's say you're the owner of a retail establishment. You "shop" your nearest competitor once every six months to determine his prices and stock. You remind yourself to do this on your calendar. You have started a regular six-month watch; you have installed a system.

Whether you are a single shopkeeper, the owner of a small business, a consultant, or an executive in a large corporation, you must be organized to benefit from information that will further your personal position. You need to be personally aware of your competition. You need the most current journals, books, directories, and other periodicals in your field. You need to make sure you are up to date.

This may seem painfully obvious, yet it is amazing to see how many otherwise sensible people fail to keep themselves informed within their own fields of interest. For example, it is estimated that there are over 400,000 consultants in the United States, but only about 10,000 of them subscribe to the trade periodicals in their individual fields.

Are You Informed?

A simple way to find out is to ask yourself these questions.

Do you belong to the principal trade or professional organization in your field? Do you take time to be active in it?

Do you subscribe to the principal trade or professional magazines in your field? Do you take the time to actually read them?

Do you periodically take the time to check up on key competitors, products, trends, government regulations, or other factors that affect you personally?

Do you at least occasionally glance through your junk mail? (It's amazing what you can learn from it!)

Do you gather information and intelligence at conferences?

Do you regularly find ways to talk to your customers and survey them?

Are you continuously alert to the types of data in your company's computers and how the data could help you?

Are you familiar with your internal information resources (your shelf of books, your company library)?

Do you have a list of outside information suppliers you can call on when necessary?

If you can't answer "yes" to all the above questions, you probably have an inadequate personal information-finding system. As a result, you probably have inadequate knowledge. Relying on friends, contacts, accountants, lawyers, and advisors is not a substitute for an information-finding system.

Moving up from the individual to the organization, the information-finding function becomes more complex, and the systems will vary, depending on the size of your organization. The steps in creating that system, however, are the same.

Whose Responsibility Should Information-Finding Be?

The first step is to decide under whose direction the principal information-finding activity will take place. In very small companies or proprietorships, it is usually the president's responsibility, or should be. In larger companies, information-finding usually falls within the marketing, planning, research and development, or library center, but is often fragmented in many different areas.

It is important to remember that information-finding and research functions can be organized by product lines, by customer groups, by sales regions, or by corporate functions. For example, product A and product B might each have its own market research department. Or there may be an information system for industrial, consumer, and government markets. Or each regional office of a company may have its own information set-up. In other organizations, the information and research operation is centralized and serves all departments, regardless of product, market, or region.

All too often, the information-finding function is buried somewhere in "administration," frequently as an adjunct of the data-processing department. This arises because of a confusion between internal and external information. A data-processing department is concerned with keeping track of a company's internal data and should not be responsible for finding external information. These are two entirely different activities.

This will change somewhat as technologies converge and companies develop top-level information executives with overall responsibility for all the information resources of an organization, both internal and external. But unless your organization has such an "information manager," the gathering of external information should be a function within the departments of those people who need external information the most, i.e., marketing, sales, research, planning, or top management.

Establishing Your Library

Once you have decided who will be responsible for the organization of the information-finding function, the next step is to establish a library or information center.

In smaller organizations, the library might be nothing more than a shelf or roomful of reference materials. These may include industry handbooks, catalogs, trade magazines, directories that cover your field, and annual reports of your customers, suppliers, and competitors. Typically, the small library should be stocked with such basic information sources as the *Thomas Register, Statistical Abstract of the United States, Business Periodicals Index, Encyclopedia of Associations, F&S Index of Corporations and Industries, Dun & Bradstreet Million Dollar Directory,* plus statistical issues of appropriate trade publications. If your mini-library will not have a full-time librarian, put a manager in charge of maintaining it. Don't expect busy secretaries to do it. This is especially true if you intend to have a computer terminal available for accessing databases and/or CD-ROMs.

The next step up is to create your own staffed internal library or information center. It could be small or large and may service anything from a law office to a large industrial complex. Such a library must be staffed by a professional librarian or information manager. This is the individual you will call upon for any and all external information. This is the person who will know how to collect information, how to disseminate it, and how to keep records.

Of course, you must have sufficient information needs to warrant the expense of having your own information center. Staffed by one professional and one assistant or clerical person, such an information center can easily cost $100,000 per year, not including overhead.

How can you tell if you need an information center? You probably do if your company is buying endless duplicate copies of books and magazines, subscribing to overlapping electronic customized news delivery services, if reference materials are piling up all over, if substantial money is being spent calling all around the United States in search of statistics, if the research being done is less than thorough, or if decisions are being delayed because of lack of information. You *definitely* need one if your employees are leaving you to work for companies with better information resources.

If you do decide to establish an information center, make sure top management is involved in its creation. Set up goals, budgets, space requirements, etc. Hire a fully qualified information professional. If you don't know how to go about this, contact a consultant or the Special Libraries Association in Washington, DC. Make sure the individual you hire is familiar with the Internet, online and CD-ROM databases and electronic document delivery services (e.g. UMI, OCLC). You want a library that will lead you forward into the twenty-first century.

Anticipating Trends

As discussed earlier in Chapter 1, the business world is changing at dizzying speeds, and the most successful firms are those that can position themselves to react quickly and flexibly to these changes as they unfold. Therefore, one of the primary duties of your library or information center should be to keep abreast of the changes that are occurring, and scoping out probable future changes—in your industry, among consumers at home and at work, with competitors, or in the external environment (such as regulatory or legal changes).

C.K. Prahalad, author of *Competing for the Future* (Harvard Business Press, 1994) says that the greatest competitive advantage a company can have is a vision of the future, and that a company's information center plays a "pivotal role" in making it happen. The reason is that the library or information center can be set up to understand the driving forces and discontinuities that are taking place. This could include trends such as the merging of distinct industries, changes taking place in the political and regulatory environment; or changes with potential customers. To identify these changes, business' need to collect this information from a wide variety of sources, and synthesize it.

How does an information center go about tracking trends and determining likely scenarios? First, you need to think of sources. Places to go for information are:

1. Print Media: Journals, books, speeches, and other traditional information sources;
2. International News and market reports; not published in the U.S.
3. Electronic discussion groups, such as newsgroups on the Internet
4. Your own circles of friends, neighbors, work colleagues, and family

Once you've tapped into these sources, you need to know what to look for. As you might imagine, spotting trends and detecting change is at least as much an art as it is a science. However, there are some specific techniques you can employ :

• Read with an open mind. Don't judge anything or form opinions initially. Just absorb information;

• Pay particular attention to what people are saying or doing; especially when it is unexpected and comes up more than once. For example, say you've read now, for the third, time about the experience of someone who has left living in a large city to move out to the country...but, decided that the tradeoffs were too great and moved back? Or, you seem to keep hearing reports about people using the Internet to stay in touch with children away at college instead of writing or calling.

• Look for what Prahalad calls "weak signals"—this is where you can say that "something" is happening—although you don't know whether it is going to become a trend. He offers an example: " a lot of companies are asking employees to work out of their homes. Now, what this will lead to we don't know, but it has implications. There are implications regarding real estate firms; implications for opportunities for offices at home; and implications for compensation." (*The Information Advisor*, October, 1994, p.3)

• Don't pay too much attention to polls and surveys. They can be extremely unreliable, have built in assumptions that bias the results, and often measure something that's occurred in the recent past, rather than a new trend. Similarly, don't put as much stock in experts opinion: you don't know their background, they may have old ways of looking at things, and again, their views may reflect recent past instead of current and future trends.

Once you've spotted what you think looks like a trend, dig deeper. Again, say you're looking at parents communicating with their children away at college over the Internet. Then, you should learn and read as much as you can about the Internet, and the dynamics of parent-child communications at college. Talk to people you know who may have children away at college: ask them if they keep in touch over the Internet: why, why not? how did they get interested in it? what do they like or not like about it?

Then, just rely on your own intelligence to synthesize this and figure out what all this might mean. Is this likely to continue? Are there some unmet needs emerging? Might this open the door to some college based Internet Service Providers to become a new, unconventional telecommunications provider? If it takes off, what does this mean for the phone companies? What sorts of other events might effect how far this trend goes: e.g. laws being considered, broader cultural changes, etc.

The winner in business for the 21st century is the one that can prepare for the future and move fastest into the best position to take advantage of the emerging opportunity. Once again, the priceless asset needed to make this happen: information.

Using an Information Broker

Unfortunately, the vast majority of organizations are simply too small to be able to afford even a small in-house library. Even companies with information centers often find their resources too limited or their staff too overburdened. Furthermore, with the amount of available information increasing, the time required to find what you need is becoming more and more costly. So whether large or small, with libraries or without, many organizations are looking for information and research assistance.

This is where the information-finding business comes in. These organizations, which are relatively new and are still evolving, gather information for you for a fee. They go by a variety of names, including "information broker," "information retailer," "fee-based information service," "information consultant," research service, and "information or knowledge retrieval service." The extent of the services of information-finding businesses varies greatly, depending on size, particular expertise, and other factors. While the smallest and most basic firms are often limited to performing online database searching and/or document retrieval services, the larger and more capable firms usually offer the following types of services:

• Access to readily available information in their own extensive, up-to-date libraries. The larger services maintain information centers containing far more reference materials than most companies could afford to purchase themselves.

• Access to a staff of highly trained and experienced consultants, researchers, and information specialists who have the expertise to track down the information you need in a rapid, cost-effective way.

• Access to a wide variety of computer databases, database vendors, CD-ROMs, and the Internet for performing wide-ranging searches on request.

• The ability to translate your questions and problems into realistic information-gathering steps. In effect, they consult with you about your needs.

• The ability to perform in-depth market studies, surveys, field interviews, and other research activities, including monitoring and current-awareness services (where you are regularly kept up to date on specific industries, companies, products, etc., of your choice).

• The ability to retrieve copies of articles, government documents, annual reports, catalogs, product samples, or whatever else you might need.

• The expertise necessary to assist you in developing—and even maintaining—your own library in conjunction with the cost-effective use of outside services.

There are large information-finding firms offering many services, and there are small outfits consisting of individual freelance researchers. A point to remember about these firms is that many offer a creative, consultative approach to information-finding, but cost significantly less than traditional consulting firms. The advantage of using an information-finding service is that all you have to do is ask the question. The firm takes it from there. But when you call such a service, try to make sure that you and they understand clearly what the question is, how extensive a search you need, when you need the results, and in what form.

As previously stated, most information-finding firms charge between $50 and $150 per hour. Some work on a project basis, others on an hourly basis. Some have retainer agreements, under which they act as your ongoing information and research service or center, responding to your daily or weekly information needs in addition to larger assignments.

We've tried to describe various possibilities for organizing an information-finding system. How should you organize yours? It obviously depends upon your requirements, but there are some general guidelines.

If your organization is small and your information needs are infrequent, you should rely mostly on information-finding firms.

If your organization is small but has frequent needs, you may want to have a small internal library plus access to one or more online vendors (like Dialog) that provide access to many databases. This setup can be supplemented by access to outside suppliers such as information-finding firms, market research companies, consultants, and the like.

If yours is a large firm with infrequent needs, you should initially do the same as infrequent users. But something may be amiss, because a large organization should need information regularly. Examine and evaluate how information is being obtained by your people. Most large firms really should have at least a small library, if only to centralize needlessly duplicated subscriptions.

11
Putting It All Together

So far, we've gone over how to ask questions. We've discussed the cost and value of information. We've shown you the new information environment. We've given you the prescription for curing information paralysis. We've tried to help you determine what sort of library and services you need. You're beginning to think like an information-conscious person. But if you're like most people, you'll want a test run. You'll want to see how it's all put together in practice.

Since everyone's information needs are different, this is difficult. But we'll take a very common information problem—the need for information on a particular industry—and go through all the steps required to solve it.

The Information Report

Assume you've developed a new type of widget. You need information on the widget industry. Assume further that you need to present this information in the form of a report.

The very first thing you should do is to find out whether anyone else has done a study on the widget industry or on any aspect of it. This would save you the trouble of researching and writing your own report. If no one has, you would then proceed to put a report together yourself by gathering all the information you need.

Your report should include:

• A description of the widget industry.

• A description and analysis of the market for widgets.

• The supplier industry structure, i.e., how the industry is organized.

• A description of the end-users or consumers.

• Factors affecting the industry/market.

Section by section, the following is what your report should cover, along with the information you should include and the questions you should be asking yourself along the way.

❑ THE INDUSTRY

Possible subsections include Introduction, History and Background, Products, Equipment, Technology, Product Applications, Trends in the Industry, and History of New Product Introductions.

The main purpose of this section is to answer a very simple question: What industry are we talking about in this report?

In most cases, this section will cover the following:

• Definition of the industry.

• History of the industry.

• Products and/or product groups that make up the industry.

• Detailed product descriptions.

• What the products are used for.

• How the products are made.

• Impact of technological developments.

• Anything special or unusual about the industry that is key to understanding it (e.g., patent expirations, profit margins, tax or tariff policies, government regulations).

Depending upon the industry, some of the items above may require full subsections. In the case of highly technical products or high-technology industries, a discussion of technology might even be contained within another main section of the report.

❏ THE MARKET

Possible subsections include Introduction, Size of the Market, Market by Product Type, Market by End-Use Sector, Sales by Outlet, and Future Trends.

This section should cover the following:

• Size of the overall market in dollars and units.

• Dollar and unit sales by product type.

• Dollar and unit sales by end-use sector.

• Dollar and unit sales by outlet.

• Imports and exports.

• Sales by region or geographic area.

For each case, figures should be given for the past five years, and projections should be given for next year, three years from now, and five years from now. Past actual growth and future projected annual growth rates should be given, with comments on the effects of inflation.

For example, let's assume the widget industry consists of steel, aluminum, and plastic widgets. Each of the three types is made by either a wet or dry process and sold through retailers, mass-merchandisers, and auto supply stores. Major users are few, consisting mostly of local governments and company fleets. A good market study will show, then, the size (in units and dollars) of the overall widget industry, and the breakdown by steel, aluminum, and plastic. A table will show sales of widgets made by wet and dry processes, broken down by steel, aluminum, and plastic, if possible. The percentage of sales of each type by outlet (retailers, mass-merchandisers, and auto supply) should be given, as well as the percentage of each type sold to the end-use market.

Of course, not all markets are ideal for this kind of breakdown, but a good study will strive for maximum breakdown and segmentation.

Figures in dollars should always be identified. Are they dollars at the manufacturer's level, wholesale level, or retail level? Are they constant dollars?

The depth of this section depends on the size, type, and scope of your needs. If your needs are limited, your budget will be, too. So your study will obviously have to rely on published data, which is sometimes good and sometimes poor. In very narrow markets, estimates frequently have to be developed. If estimates have to be developed for most of the market size tables, it is rare that such estimates can be made for past years, so it is better to concentrate on figures for the current year and future years.

Studies performed very early or very late in a year should include estimates. For example, a study done in late 1995 or early 1996 will usually include reliable figures for 1994, but figures may not yet be available for 1995. The study should make sure estimates for 1995 are included, as well as projections for 1996.

This section of your report should make ample use of charts and tables, and the text should summarize the key points in the tables as well as discuss trends and growth rates.

The success of your report will almost always hinge on how well organized and complete this section is. This is especially true for studies requiring estimates (due to the lack of secondary data).

There are some pitfalls to be aware of:

• Domestic consumption of a product is usually measured by manufacturers' shipments, plus imports, less exports. This may not be true in industries where retailers or wholesalers keep very large inventories, or when an impending strike causes an inventory build-up.

• When the market consists largely of imports, it is vital to understand how much the value of the landed import (including duty) is marked up by the importer before he sells it to a wholesaler, distributor, or retailer.

• Secondary sources can be inaccurate or misleading in identifying the size of the market in terms of manufacturer's or retail dollars. One source consistently identifies its figures for certain industries as being "factory shipments" or "factory-level dollars," but close examination reveals that imports are included.

• The definition of product categories in one source may differ. For example, if the United States government had import figures for widgets, the particular widgets included might be different from those included in a magazine's figures for sales of widgets.

❏ SUPPLIER INDUSTRY STRUCTURE

Possible subsections include Introduction, Competition or Companies in the Field, Pricing, Margins and Markups, Distribution Methods, Advertising and Promotion, and Company Profiles.

Once the size of the market has been covered, and you know how much of each product is sold through what outlets and to whom, the next step is to describe the suppliers or manufacturers of the products—who are they, where do they stand in relation to one another, and how do they bring their products to the marketplace?

The most important objective of this section is to identify the leading companies in the field and their respective share of the market. Some historical perspective on their marketshare position should also be provided.

The competitive situation can usually be covered in one of two ways. In the less expensive studies, or for industries dominated by just a few companies, the general description of each company and the marketshare data can usually be covered in one section of the report. In more in-depth studies or in those covering major industries, it is often necessary to augment such a section with a separate section called Company Profiles, in which each company is described in detail.

If there is no company profile section, then the section on the competition should include at least:

- Identification of major and secondary companies in the field.
- Their sales of the product(s) in dollars and, if possible, in units.
- Their current marketshare position and historical trends.
- Major differences between the companies in terms of management, manufacturing processes, marketing methods, etc.
- Major differences in product lines, product types, etc.
- Major competitive trends.

If a company profile section *is* included, it is then possible to go into further detail on each company. Such details may include:

- Names of top management.
- Complete description of product(s) within the industry being covered.
- Dollar sales of company as a whole and for product(s) being covered.
- Profitability of product(s).
- Important parent/subsidiary relationships.
- Manufacturing facilities, methods, and cost factors.
- Availability of resources.
- Labor contracts.
- Company organization, marketing philosophy, and practices.
- Franchises and international operations.
- New products; research and development expenditures.
- Technological advantages or disadvantages.

Structuring a market study is complicated by both the inclusion and exclusion of company profiles. If there are no profiles, the section describing the competitive situation and different companies in the industry can get bogged down in details on each company. If there are profiles, inserting them immediately after a Summary of Competition section can interrupt the flow of the study. Thus, if company profiles are included, it is often wise to include them as an appendix or as a separate section at the end of the report.

Some in-depth reports (especially those done for acquisition purposes) may require even greater depth of information about some or all of the major companies in the field. Such information might include actual operation financial figures, organization charts, locations of plants, biographies of key principals, a bibliography of articles about each company, clippings of the company's advertising, copies of annual reports or 10-K's, etc. Generally, all of these should be included as appendices and not written into the main body of the study.

Of course, the depth of information required on each company will depend mostly on the depth and cost of the study as a whole.

Whatever the budget, however, a frequent error made in many studies is the failure to include at least a list of the major and secondary competing companies with their correct names and addresses and the brand names of their products. For example, assume a leading product in the widget industry is called Widgetco and that it is distributed in the United States by a company called the American Widget Company. Assume that the American Widget Company only assembles Widgetco, and that the parts are actually made in Germany by the International Widget Company, which happens to own 80 percent of the American Widget Company. All of this information should be made very clear in the study, and the list of producers should include both the American Widget Company and its parent, the International Widget Company.

The section on the supplier industry structure should also cover pricing, distribution methods, and advertising and promotion. Usually, these will make up three different subsections, but that will depend on the individual study.

The subsection on pricing should give a sense of the price ranges of the various product categories. Such a section can also include one of the key areas of a good market study—a detailed discussion of margins and markups. What is the manufacturer's profit margin? How much are the products marked up at each level in the distribution process?

The subsection on distribution should provide a complete description of the methods of distribution used in the industry, including any differences between the methods of the industry leaders. Here's a list of typical items to be covered:

• Description of manufacturer's sales organization: Are the products sold by salespersons? If so, how? How many salespersons? How are territories divided?

• Role of warehouses, if any.

• Roles of wholesalers, jobbers, representatives, agents, importers: Is distribution accomplished mainly through any of these? If so, how? Which major manufacturer uses which? What are the payment terms, commission rates, markups? How much control do manufacturers have over representatives? What is the training of representatives and agents?

• Role of retailers: What are the major types of retail outlets used? What is the role of mass merchandisers, catalogs, showrooms? What are their geographical distribution? What are retailers' expected yearly turnovers? What is the retail markup and profit margin? What are the payment terms? Are there any discounts? Is there price cutting? Are there any co-op advertising allowances? Is there any merchandising?

A very extensive study might include as appendices a table of all products and recent retail prices; a map showing geographical distribution of warehouses, retail outlets, and wholesalers; charts showing sales or distribution organizations; specific documents showing agreements between manufacturers and distributors; etc.

The subsection on advertising and promotion should explain how the industry talks to its end-users. What advertising media are being used, how much is being spent overall, and what are the sales messages being conveyed? Appendix support for this section might include details of advertising expenditure by company for the past several years, tear sheets of actual ads, transcripts of television or radio ads, packaging types, lists of industry periodicals and trade shows, copies of pages from their Internet web sites, etc.

❏ END-USERS/CONSUMERS

Possible subsections include Introduction, Market Potential and Penetration, Typical End-User, Consumer Demographics, and Consumer Surveys.

The exact title and organization of this section of your report depends, obviously, on whether your widgets are sold to businesses or consumers or both.

While many studies offer a good assessment of the present size of the market in terms of dollar and unit sales of the products, few studies really discuss the potential size of the market and the current penetration. For example, it is valuable to know how many widgets are being sold this year, but it is also valuable to know how many potential users of widgets there are in the marketplace and how many widgets are actually out there being used.

This section should cover the following:

• Who buys the product(s) covered in this study? If businesses, what kind of business? Who is the key individual buyer? If consumers, what are their demographics, characteristics?

• Why is the product purchased or not purchased?

• What are the economic factors involved? (Disposable income, inflation, recession, etc.)

• What are the psychological factors involved in the purchasing decision?

- Where and how do end-users buy the product(s)?
- Any trends in end-users/consumers?

In many cases, the results of published surveys of end-users/consumers are available, and these should obviously be summarized within the text of the report. If an end-user survey was performed expressly for the report, then its results would be very prominently featured and discussed.

Demographic profiles of consumers (especially for products sold in supermarkets) are frequently available.

❏ FACTORS AFFECTING THE INDUSTRY/MARKET

Possible subsections include Government Regulations, World Conditions, New Technology, Strikes, and Embargoes.

This section should cover any factors that influence the industry or market. In most cases, government regulations (their description and impact) will be the major factors discussed.

Getting the Information for Your Report

Once you've outlined the information you need, you now have to go out and find it.

The easiest thing to do would be to hire an information-finding, research, or consulting firm, or some other information supplier, to find the information for you. But if you'd rather do it yourself, here's a checklist—by no means all-inclusive—of thirteen steps to take. Many of these steps can be applied to virtually any information need:

1. As previously mentioned, find out whether anyone has already done a study on the subject. If someone has, and it contains even some of the information you need, you've saved yourself a lot of money.
2. Perform a five-year retrospective search of published litera-

ture (articles, etc.) on widgets, using both computer databases and manual methods. Then, retrieve the full text of all the relevant articles you find referenced or summarized in the databases and indices. Depending on the industry, keep in mind that major overview articles about an industry are occasionally missed if they have appeared in publications that are not indexed or not well indexed.

3. Contact the widget industry association, if there is one, and have it send you whatever information may be relevant. If there is no association, find out whether there are associations in related fields.

4. Obtain data on advertising expenditures by companies making widgets. There are commercial information services that do this (e.g., Leading National Advertisers, Inc., in New York City). The reason this is important is that it will help you identify those companies that are actively advertising their widgets and how much they spend on advertising. This can help define the size of their operations.

5. If your widgets are going to be sold to consumers, you should immediately obtain whatever information may be available from audit firms like A.C. Nielsen Company (Chicago, Illinois). Note that this data will be expensive, but it's worth it.

6. Make sure you get the technical specifications and product descriptions, as well as product catalogues, on competitive widget products. Any patent information can be obtained from the United States government. Catalogs are very useful information sources and can often be obtained simply by calling the individual companies. There are also a variety of commercial information services that have product information.

7. Check Wall Street investment firms to see if they've written reports on either the widget industry or individual companies in the industry. These reports, written for investment advisory purposes, often contain much valuable research information. Many of these firms no longer give these reports away free, but they are generally available from the

firms themselves, from distributors like FIND/SVP, or from databases like *Investext*.

8. Get data on imports and exports of widgets from the Department of Commerce.

9. Get all relevant data on the widget industry from the *Census of Manufacturers* and other United States government publications.

10. Get any data on widgets from such sources as *Standard & Poor's Industry Surveys*, annual issues of periodicals, and any other guides and directories. Don't forget to check whether any books have been written on widgets; refer to *Books in Print* (R.R. Bowker.)

11. Order tear sheets of advertisements on widgets. There are services—like Advertising Information Services in New York City—that will do this for you. You can also obtain copies of television and radio commercials if necessary.

12. From the foregoing, plus any industry directories or general directories like the *Thomas Register of American Manufacturers*, make a list of all companies in the industry and begin gathering the company data:

   • Annual report, if available. Call the company to get it.

   • Copies of all Securities and Exchange Commission filings, if the company is public.

   • Product catalogs.

   • Literature on the parent/subsidiary relationships.

   • Literature on the major companies in the field.

   • Dun & Bradstreet reports on privately held companies.

   • Any available marketshare information on individual companies or manufacturing plants, obtained with the help of services or databases.

13. Finally, you'll want to check out appropriate Internet sources like the web sites of companies in the industry.

While this is by no means an exhaustive list of secondary research techniques, it does cover the basic steps essential to getting information on an industry. Once you have gathered all of this information, you should have a pretty good picture of the widget business.

Primary Research

Now you're ready for primary research, that is, interviews with industry sources, companies, end-users, etc.

From the information gathered, it is usually possible to identify a number of possible experts on the industry. These can be authors of major articles in the trade press, or they can be individuals in associations or people who are quoted frequently in the articles you have gathered. These people can usually be called and interviewed about trends and developments that have not yet been reported.

Next, you should conduct telephone and—where possible—in-person interviews with manufacturers, wholesalers, distributors, and retailers of widgets.

How much will all this cost? How long will it take?

It depends, of course, on the type of industry and market being examined. If an outside firm does the work for you, you can figure that a complete, thorough examination of an industry would require at least two months' time and would cost between $15,000 and $50,000, not including a survey of consumers or end-users. Such a survey might add anywhere from $15,000 to $75,000 to the cost, depending on the size of the respondent sample surveyed, the number of questions asked, the tabulations required, etc.

On the other hand, if you elected to do the same report completely by yourself, it could possibly take you two or three times as long, not including the survey of consumers or end-users. Thus, if you earn $50,000 a year and it takes you six months of full-time work, the cost would be $25,000 of your time. Of course, this wouldn't include your opportunity cost—the money you have lost by spending six months on research.

Conclusion

The return on an investment in information is knowledge.

We hope that your return on the investment of reading this book is a higher level of information consciousness.

At this point, you should understand at least the basic steps involved in becoming a better-informed individual—in your business and personal life. You should know how to ask the right kinds of questions, and how to think about ways to find information that may be hard to get.

Ideally, you now have a solid understanding of the sources of information available to you today, how to find and use them, and how to put information to work for your business and career.

Being well informed brings success. Watch how quickly the lights turn green for you at every juncture because of your new state of preparation. Notice how much time you save—and think about the value of that time to you. And ponder the benefits of enlightenment.

Appendix I
Key "Sources of Sources"

The following is a selected listing of some of the best and most comprehensive business information "sources of sources." These list and/or analyze thousands of different sources of business information, and are therefore some of the most important resources in any business library. Because these sources are so all-encompassing, they can often be used as first places to check when undertaking any information search.

American Library Directory
R.R. Bowker
Reed Reference Publishing
121 Chanlon Road
New Providence, NJ 07974

This is a leading guide to public and academic libraries throughout the United States.

Books in Print
R.R. Bowker
Reed Reference Publishing
121 Chanlon Road
New Providence, NJ 07974

This is the guide to finding out about published books. Volumes include a title, subject, and author directory, as well as one that lists names, addresses, and phone numbers for thousands of publishers.

Burwell's World Directory of Information Brokers
Burwell Enterprises
3724 FM 1960 West, Suite 214
Houston, TX 77068

This leading paperbound directory lists all the known "information bro-

kers" and information-finding services throughout the United States and around the world. Each entry includes a contact name and number, subject specialties, and other useful information.

Business Information Sources
3rd Edition, 1993
Lorna M. Daniells
University of California Press
2120 Berkeley Way
Berkeley, CA 94720

This is one of the most well-known business reference guides ever published, and a classic in its field. Daniells is the retired head of Harvard University's Graduate School of Business Administration's Baker Library. Her book describes and analyzes all of the major business books, reference sources, bibliographies, indices, directories, statistic sources, and more.

Consultants and Consulting Organizations Directory
Gale Research Company
835 Penobscot Building
Detroit, MI 48226

This is the leading directory of consultants in the United States. It includes geographic as well as major subject indices.One caution is that the directory does not have useful criteria for qualifying expertise.

Directories in Print
Gale Research Company
835 Penobscot Building
Detroit, MI 48226

A superb "directory of directories," this book is often an excellent "first stop" when initiating an information search.

Directory of Special Libraries and Information Centers
Gale Research Company
835 Penobscot Building
Detroit, MI 48226

This is an extensive, authoritative guide to "special" libraries—nontraditional libraries that specialize in particular subjects.

Encyclopedia of Associations
Gale Research Company
835 Penobscot Building
Detroit, MI 48226

This is an invaluable guide to professional associations throughout the United States, which are typically excellent sources of statistics and expertise. Companion directories are available for state and regional associations, as well as for international associations.

The Encyclopedia of Business Information Sources
Gale Research Company
835 Penobscot Building
Detroit, MI 48226

This directory presents a wide range of business information sources listed under 1,000 alphabetical business subjects. It includes databases, publications, organizations, etc.

Findex: The Directory of Market Research Reports, Studies, and Surveys
Cambridge Information Group
7200 Wisconsin Avenue.
Bethesda, MD 20814

This is a very useful directory listing available market research reports, a full description of each report, and pricing and ordering information. You can search this directory online on Dialog and other services.

The Fiscal Directory of Fee-Based Information Research and Document Supply Services
American Library Association
50 E. Huron Street
Chicago IL 60611

This very useful and inexpensive guide lists information services as well as document delivery services for over 200 libraries and information centers throughout the United States.

Gale Directory of Publications and Broadcast Media
Gale Research Company
835 Penobscot Building
Detroit, MI 48226

A leading guide to finding the names and addresses of thousands of publications and publishers throughout the United States.

Gale Guide to Internet Databases
Gale Research Company
835 Penobscot Building
Detroit, MI 48226

Although it is nearly impossible to compile a comprehensive, up to date print directory of Internet sites, Gale's guide is a useful overview of some of the most important searchable databases on the Internet, and is quite easy to use and understand, especially if you are a newcomer to the Internet.

Information Industry Directory
Information Industry Association
555 New Jersey Avenue
Washington DC 20001

This annual guide lists organizations, publications, and services involved in producing and disseminating electronic information and is very useful if you are studying the make-up of the information industry.

Information Sources
Information Industry
Association
555 New Jersey Avenue NW
Washington, DC 20001

This directory is published by the leading professional association of major information companies and organizations. It is a "who's who" of those companies, describing what they publish, names of key executives, and other important data.

Lesko's Info-Power
Information USA Inc.
PO Box E.
Kensington, MD 20895

Written by nationally-known expert Matthew Lesko, Info Power is chock full of names, addresses, phone numbers and contacts for locating experts within the federal government and other official bodies.

**Monthly Catalog of
United States Government
Publications**
U.S. Government Printing
Office
Washington, DC 20402

One of the standard references for keeping up with what the United States government is publishing, this volume is arranged alphabetically and has an index.

**Oxbridge Directory of
Newsletters**
Oxbridge Communications
150 Fifth Avenue
New York, NY 10011

This is a leading directory for finding names and contact information for the tens of thousands of specialized newsletters published throughout the United States.

Research Centers Directory
Gale Research Company
835 Penobscot Building
Detroit, MI 48226

This is a fascinating directory that lists and describes organizations that conduct research on thousands of different topics.

Standard Periodical Directory
Oxbridge Communications
150 Fifth Avenue
Suite 236
New York, NY 10011

This is another leading directory of magazines and periodicals published throughout the United States.

Subject Collections
R.R. Bowker
Reed Reference Publishing
121 Chanlon Road
New Providence NJ 07974

Organized by subject, this is a guide to special collections of university, college, public, and special libraries in the United States.

Ulrich's International Periodicals Directory
R.R. Bowker
Reed Reference Publishing
121 Chanlon Road
New Providence, NJ 07974

This is an extensive guide to 130,000 periodicals published throughout the world.

United States Government Manual
Superintendent of Documents
Government Printing Office
Washington, DC 20402

This is the official guide to the organization, services, and resources of all of the departments, agencies, and quasi-governmental entities in the United States. It is an excellent manual for understanding how the government is set up, and where to go for information.

Washington Information Directory
Congressional Quarterly
1414 22nd St. NW
Washington, DC 20037

This excellent guide to information resources located in Washington, DC includes both public and private sources.

Yahoo!
Internet Address:
http://www.yahoo.com

Not a print directory, but the best known of the Internet information finding tools. Yahoo! is an easy to use and highly regarded index that can help you locate what you need on the Internet. (Other excellent Internet search utilities include InfoSeek (http://www.infoseek.com) and Open Text (http://www.opentext.com)

Appendix II
Directories of Databases and Online Services

The following is a list of major guides to currently available databases and online services:

Bibliodata Fulltext Sources Online
Bibliodata Inc.
PO Box 61
Needham Heights, MA.02194

Not a database directory per se, but a very useful and well organized compilation of where to locate online the fulltext of various information sources such as magazines and journals.

Federal Database Finder
Information USA
PO Box E
Kensington MA 20895

Identifies and describes 4,200 databases and files available to the public from the United States government.

Find it Online!
Windcrest/McGraw-Hill
Blue Ridge Summit, PA

Find it Online! provides a basic introduction on how to do research online, and is written by this book's co-author Robert Berkman. Find it Online! describes and compares consumer online services, CD-ROMs, the Internet, and other electronic information sources.

Gale Directory of Databases
Gale Research Company
Penobscot Building
Detroit, MI 48226

This is the most comprehensive guide to databases, published by Gale, the leading information reference book publisher. Volume 1 covers 5,300 databases available online; volume 2 lists 3,500 CD-ROM, and other portable databases. Also provides information on over 3,300 database producers and approximately 700 database vendors.

CD-ROM Directories:

The CD-ROM Directory
TFPL
22 Peter's Lane
London UK EC1M 6DS

This directory lists over 6,000 CD-ROM titles from around the world.

The CD-ROM Finder
Information Today Inc.
143 Old Marlton Pike
Medford NJ 08055

1995 6th Edition; covers about 2,300 titles covered.

CD-ROMs in Print
Gale Research Company
Penobscot Building
Detroit, MI 48226

Another leading directory of CD-ROMS, this one also includes a variety of indexes for locating producers and distributors.

Gale Directory of Databases: Vol 2
Gale Research Company
Penobscot Building
Detroit, MI 48226

See Description above under Gale Directory of Databases)

Major Online Services:

The following is a list of some of the major online vendors of interest to business. This is not an all-inclusive list by any means, but does identify those vendors most prominent in the industry. The first section lists professional business database providers and the second section the consumer oriented services.

ADP Network Services, Inc.
175 Jackson Plaza
Ann Arbor, MI 48106
(313) 769-6800

ADP specializes in a wide range of economic and financial databases, and has the capacity to forecast and model the data.

Bloomberg
Bloomberg Financial Network
499 Park Avenue
New York, NY 10022
(212) 318-2000

Bloomberg is a fast growing and aggressive provider of a wide variety of business and financial news, available not just online, but via several different formats.

CIFAR
Center for International
Financial Analysis and
Research
3490 U.S. Highway 1; BL012
Princeton, NJ 08540
(609) 520-9333

"Cifarbase" provides current and historical financial data for over 7,000 companies; 2,600 of them are European-based.

Commission of the European Communities (ECHO)
B.P. 2373
L-10231
Luxembourg
352-34981 200
Fax: 352 34981 234

The European Community has created a series of databases, many of which are free, that are designed to provide information and advice on the European Community single market.

CompuServe, Inc.
5000 Arlington Center Blvd.
Columbus, OH 43220
(614) 457-8600
(800) 848-8990

This popular system provides general and business articles, brokerage reports, stock quotes, company data, electronic bulletin boards, and other consumer and business information.

Data Resources Inc.(DRI)/ McGraw-Hill
24 Hartwell Avenue
Lexington, MA 02173
(617) 863-5100

DRI specializes in databases covering economics and economic forecasts.

Data-Star
485 Devon Park Drive
Suite 110
Wayne, PA 19087
(800) 221-7754

Data-Star is a European-based host accessible in the United States via telecommunication gateways. Data-Star has a number of unique databases that provide key facts and analyses on European companies and industries.

DataTimes
14000 Quail Springs Parkway
Suite 450
Oklahoma City, OK 73134
(800) 642-2525

DataTimes has been well known in the professional online industry for its fulltext newspapers online, but most recently has introduced a more business consumer oriented search system called EyeQ that offers a graphical interface and low search fees.

Dialog
Knight-Ridder Information Inc.
2440 El Camino Real
Mountain View CA 94040
(415) 858-3785
(800) 334-2564

Dialog is the leading online database host, and currently makes available over 450 databases, covering a very wide subject range. Subjects covered include agriculture, biochemistry, biotechnology, chemicals, company statistics, computer science, defense and aerospace, education, electronics, engineering, energy, environment, finance, government, humanities, international business, labor, market research, materials science, medicine, mergers and acquisitions, news, patents, packaging technology, petroleum, pharmaceuticals, physics, psychology, public affairs, regulations, safety, science and technology, social science, tax and accounting, toxicology, tradenames, and much more!

Dow Jones News/Retrieval
PO Box 300
Princeton, NJ 08543
(609) 520-4000

Dow Jones provides online access to extremely current business and financial news, as well as information on sports and weather. Currently Dow Jones offers about 75 databases on their system, including the Asian Wall Street Journal, Dow Jones Business and Finance Report, SEC Online, Wall Street Week, Zacks Earnings & Estimates, and many more.

Individual Inc.
8 New England Executive
Park West
Burlington MA 01803
(800) 766-4224

Not really a database provider, Individual Inc. specializes in providing customized electronic news delivery to the businesspersons desktop PC. It also offers a low cost version over the web at: http://www.newspage.com

Interactive Market Systems, Inc.
11 West 42nd Street
New York, NY 10036
(212) 789-3600

A basic tool for the advertising and marketing industries, this host provides information on forecasting, media mix, reach and frequency, market research, and television and radio ratings.

Lexis-Nexis
PO Box 933
Dayton, OH 45401
(513) 865-6800
(800) 543-6862

Lexis-Nexis is well-known in the online industry as a provider of full-text access to a wide range of both legal information (on its Lexis database) and general and business news (on its Nexis database).

National Data Corporation
Corporate Financial Services Division
Corporate Square
Atlanta, GA 30329
(404) 329-8500

National Data Corporation's concentration is in the banking and investment information areas.

National Library of Medicine
Medlars Management Section
8600 Rockville Pike
Bethesda, MD 20894
(301) 496-6193
(800) 638-8480

Over thirty databases in the health sciences are available from the National Library of Medicine. Major topics include toxicology, general medicine, cancer, and hospital management.

NewsNet Inc.
945 Haverford Road
Bryn Mawr, PA 19010
(215) 527-8030
(800) 345-1301

NewsNet accesses the full text of hundreds of specialized newsletters in many subject areas. Often, the electronic versions of newsletters are available before the print versions.

OCLC
6565 Frantz Road
Dublin, OH 43026
(800) 345-1301

OCLC is well known in the library market, as it offers several popular news and publication indexes online, as well as databases useful for librarians and researchers.

Profile Information: FT Profile
Financial Times
Bracken House
10 Cannon Street
London EC 4P, England

FT Profile has strong European coverage and a number of databases devoted specifically to the 1992 European single market.

Profound Inc.
655 Madison Avenue
New York, NY 10022
(212) 750-6900

Profound offers indepth business news, market reports, country studies, company backgrounds and stock quotes in full graphical format and is geared to nonprofessional searchers.

Questel/Orbit
8000 Westpark Drive
McLean, VA 22102
(800) 456-7248

Questel/Orbit's main area of specialty is providing information about patents and related areas

Telmar Group
148 Madison Avenue
New York, NY 10016
(212) 725-3000

Telmar supports research efforts for advertising and marketing by offering such databases as ABC Newspaper Circulation, Arbitron, Nielsen, PMB, and others.

Thomson Financial Services
Investext Group
22 Pittsburgh Street
Boston, MA 02110
(617) 345-2000

Best known for its Investext database of investment analysis reports, Thomson also makes a variety of research studies are reports available online to its own subscribers.

University Microfilms Inc. (UMI)
Investext Group

22 Pittsburgh Street
Boston, MA 02110
(617) 345-2000

Long time publisher and indexer UMI has moved into the online database field with its ProQuest Direct, which is a Windows-based system that allows for easy online searching and downloading of full graphical images.

West Publishing
620 Opperman Drive
Eagan, MN 55123
(800) 328-9352

West is well known in the professional research community for its comprehensive offering of government, regulatory, tax and law databases.

Consumer Online Services:

America Online
8619 Westwood Center Drive
Vienna, VA 22182
(800) 827-6364

America Online is better known for its rapid growth, top notch graphics, and ease of use then it is for its depth of business information offerings. However, America Online offers its users an easy to use web browser for accessing the world wide web on the Internet.

Compuserve Inc.
5000 Arlington Centre
Boulevard

PO Box 20212
Columbus OH 43220
(800) 848-8199

Out of all the consumer online services, Compuserve offers the greatest number and most comprehensive business databases. Its Knowledge Index service is actually a low-cost subset of the Dialog professional online service.

Microsoft Network

Microsoft Corp
One Microsoft Way
Redmond, WA 98052
(206)882-8080

Microsoft has signed up several traditional business information providers, such as Dun & Bradstreet. It is the newest—and the most closely watched—of the consumer online services.

Prodigy Services Company

445 Hamilton Avenue
White Plains, NY 10601
(914)448-8000

Prodigy has never had much of a reputation for offering indepth business information, but it does offer some very good world wide web browsing tools, as well as some handy personal financial and investment services.

Appendix III
The Best Business Research Web Sites

Although there are literally thousands of business related sites on the Internet and the world wide web, only a small percentage actually contain useful, substantive business research information. What we've done here is provide you with a sampling of what we feel are some of the very best and most useful sites. The first part identifies pointers and clearinghouses—these are sites that will lead you to other sites. Part two is a list of what we have found to be some of the very best business sites themselves. The last section provides the web addresses of the best and most popular web search engines.

Keep in mind that although all of the following sites were working and active as of late 1995, the web is a very volatile area, and sites come and go rapidly. Also, although all of the following sources are free of charge, sometimes firms will initiate an Internet site for free, but begin charging fees later.

Part 1: Pointers and Clearinghouses

Name of Site/Source	Sample Links/Contents	Web Address
The CIO Help Desk (Entex Information Services)	CIA World Factbook Library of Congress SEC EDGAR Database	http://www.entex-is.com/ DOCBIZ/HTML
Find/SVP Top Business Information Centers (Find/SVP)	CEO Access CommerceNet Harvard Business Review	http://www.findsvp.com
Carol's Guide to Reference Sources (Carol Oakes, Reference Librarian, Boise State Univ.)	Well researched and organized links to business reference and related material. See especially "International Business Sources" for links to statistical sources, exporting, country data, etc.	http://www.idbsu.edu/carol/
Business Oriented Information (Charm Net)	See "The Commerce Page" for links to resources such as stock quotes, economic data, Dun & Bradstreet, etc.	http://www.charm.net/biz.html
Thomas Ho's Favorite Electronic Commerce WWW resources (Thomas Ho)	Large, well organized list of resource covering a wide range of topics. See in particular "directories and clearinghouses" for locating firms on the web.	http://www.engr.iupui.edu/ ~ho/interests/commmenu.htm
A Business Researcher's Interests (Yogest Malhorta, University of Pittsburgh.)	Comprehensive, well thought out list of business research related information covering areas such as: Business/technology university sites; Intellectual property, legal & policy issues.	http://www.pitt.edu/~malhorta/ interest2.html
FINWEB (University of Texas)	A comprehensive collection of business and finance links.	http://www.finweb.com
U.S. Bureau of the Census (U.S. Bureau of the Census)	Provides links to key census data	http://www.census.gov

Name of Site/Source	Sample Links/Contents	Web Address
Global Network Navigator: Business & Finance (Global Network Navigator)	Links to topics related to agriculture, business, employment, government, investment, management, marketing, real estate and more.	http://nearnet.gnn.com/wic/bus.53.html

Part 2: Best Business Information Sources

Name of Source/Provider	Description/Contents	Web Address
9th Revision Directory of Scholarly Electronic Conferences/ Business, Accounting, Finance and Marketing (Leslie Haas)	Extremely valuable and thorough listing of Internet discussion groups related to business. Includes description and contact addresses.	http://www.lib.umich.edu/chhome.thm
Commercial Services on the Net (Open Market)	Allows keyword and Boolean searching to find companies and products on the web.	http://www.directory.net/
National Trade Data Bank (U.S. Dept. of Commerce)	Massive collection of world trade data produced by U.S. Department of Commerce	http://www.stat-usa.gov/ben.html
CIA World Fact Book (U.S. Central Intelligence Agency)	Provides descriptive and statistical data on 264 nations around world.	http://www.ic.gov
LabStat (U.S.Bureau of Labor Statistics)	Statistics on employment and labor such as unemployment, consumer spending, etc.	http://stats.bls.gov
Hoover's Online (The Reference Press)	Nicely designed web site that offers free links to over 1,000 corporate web presences.	http://www.hoovers.com/bizreg.html
EDGAR (Taxpayer's Assett Project)	Interactive searching of the EDGAR SEC filings database	http://www.sec.gov/edgarhp.html

Name of Source/Provider	Description/Contents	Web Address
MIT's Stock Price Charts (Massachusetts Institute of Technology)	Provides recent stock market information, including previous day's closing prices and one-year graphs of historical prices.1	http://www.ai.mit.edu/stocks.htm
Knight Ridder Financial News (Knight-Ridder, Inc.)	A service of Asia, Inc Online, this site provides timely and useful world-wide stock and financial headlines and news.	http://www.asia-inc.com/knight/index.html
CorpTech Technology Registry (Corporate Technology Information Systems Inc.)	Indepth, substantive reports on a variety of technology sectors and markets, such as biotechnology, computers, medical, and more.	http://www.batnet.com:80/techreg/corptech.html
Thomas Register of American Manufacturers (Thomas Publishing)	Locate information on companies that offer a product or service (not necessarily on the Internet)	http://www.thomasregister.com/8000/
Quick Quotes QuoteCom	Search for current stock quotes. Free, but user must registerl	http://www.quote.com/quot.htm
Fortune Magazine	Fortune articles, a searchable Fortune 500 database, and other business news and reports.	http://www.pathfinder.com/fortune/
PR Newswire (PR Newswire)	Free searchable file of news from public and private firms, government agencies, and various organizations.	http://www.prnewswire.com
STO's Internet Patent Search (Source Translation & Optimization—STO)	System allows user to determine patent class, retrieve patent titles and abstracts, receive patent documentation, and more	http://sunsite.unc.edu/patents/intropat.html

Part 3: Internet Search Engines

The following is a list of some of the most popular and useful search engines on the Internet. These allow you to better target what you need to find on the net by letting you perform keyword searches of web sites and other parts of the Internet.

Alta Vista

This search engine, introduced by Digital Equipment Corporation in February, 1996, is very fast and powerful. It searches both web pages and usenet discussion groups, and offers an "advanced search" mode that allows for use of Boolean operators.

Address:
http://www.altavista.digital.com

Deja News

Unlike the other search engines listed here, this one does not search web sites, but specializes in searching the fulltext of the usenet newsgroup postings. By using this search engine, you can read recent posts from newsgroups without having to subscribe to the groups yourself.

Address:
http://www.dejanews.com

Savvy Search

This search engine is actually a "meta" search engine, which will simultaneously search multiple search engines. It is most useful for locating very obscure and hard to find information.

Address: http://www.savvy-search.com

Lycos

Lycos, a search engine from Carnegie Mellon University, is reported to contain a database of three million URL's (web addresses). Users receive a short but descriptive summary of each web site retrieved. There is no full Boolean searching, but Lycos allows for use of word segments and will even search for "similar" words to the keywords provided.

Address:
http://lycos.cs.cmu.edu/

Excite

This search engine is a product of Architect Software. Its claim to fame is that it not only searches the full-text of about 1.5 million web pages, but also provides a searchable database of net site reviews.

Address: http://www.excite.com

Yahoo

Unlike the above search tools, Yahoo is a manually created index, and provides a hierarchal cascading index of web sites and usenet groups, organized by subject. It also contains a search tool that performs keyword searches of all the documents and URLs in the yahoo file. Yahoo has been one of the most popular free search tools on the net, and while as of this writing is still free, has been sold to a private enterprise and now includes advertisements.

Address:
http://www.yahoo.com

Open Text Corporation

Open Text has received much acclaim as an Internet search engine that allows for more sophisticated searching, not typically available on the Internet. For example, you can specify how far apart your keywords should be located, and in which section of the web pages.

Address:
http://www.opentext.com

Infoseek

Infoseek searches not only web sites but the usenet discussion groups as well, which can be a powerful tool for finding out what people are saying and discussing on everything from your industry, your product, competitors, social issues of the day, consumer problems, and so on. Infoseek allows the use of keyword searching with Boolean operators, and utilizes relevancy

ranking software to make matches. Although a basic level of searching is free, you can pay a monthly fee to InfoSeek for more advanced capabilities.

Address:
http://www.infoseek.com

NlightN: The Library Corporation

This ambitious project actually goes beyond "just" searching the Internet and is, according to the President of The Library Corporation, designed to provide "access to all formal information." Currently its scope includes hundreds of online databases, three million web documents from Lycos' web crawler (see above), and 14 newswires. The databases are drawn from a wide selection, and include well-known files such as ABI/Inform, UnCover, the GPO, Journal Graphics, H.W. Wilson files, and many more. To search nlightn you type in a query, and if you choose, employ Boolean operators and parentheses, and the system uses its "universal index" to search the fulltext of all its files Like InfoSeek, the firm offers a basic level of service free, but charges for more advanced capabilities and for a document retrieval service.

Address:
http://www.nlightn.com

Appendix IV
Information-Finding Companies

The following is a list of some of the largest and leading information-finding services. This list is not all-inclusive by any means, and is restricted to the larger commercial organizations. (For a much more comprehensive listing of both large and small information-gathering firms, see the reference to *Burwell's World Directory of Information Brokers* in Appendix I. Most of the below firms offer more than one of the following services: information finding, consulting, competitive intelligence, custom market research, computer database searching, and document retrieval.

Fuld & Company
Cambridge, MA

FIND/SVP
New York, NY

Information Store
Berkeley, CA

Michael M. Kaiser and Associates
Arlington, CA

Kirk Tyson International
Oak Brook, IL

Research on Demand
Berkeley, CA

Strategic Information Services
New York, NY

Teltech Resource Network Corporation
Minneapolis, MN

Washington Researchers
Washington, DC

In addition to the above services, a number of academic and public libraries have established divisions that offer computer database searching and/or certain information retrieval services to the public for a fee. An excellent directory of these services is *The Fiscal Directory of Fee-Based Information Services in Libraries,* published by FYI at the Los Angeles Public Library in Norwalk, California.

Appendix V
How-To Books and Guides

The following is a list of books that explain how to perform marketing and other forms of research. Some are standard texts; others are more specialized.

This appendix is broken down into three sections:

1. general research texts.
2. market research texts.
3. competitive intelligence books and guides.

GENERAL RESEARCH TEXTS:

Business Information: How to Find it, How to Use It
2nd Edition, 1992
Oryx Press
Phoenix, AZ

Author Michael Lavin does an excellent job not only in pointing out where to find sources of business information, but also in offering valuable advice on how to best interpret data and be a smarter user of business information.

Find it Fast: How to Uncover Expert Information on Any Subject
HarperCollins
10 East 53rd Street
New York, NY 10022

The third edition of this reference book was published in 1994 and is written by this book's co-author Robert Berkman. It identifies and describes various sources of information, analyzes how to perform business research, and advises how to find and interview subject experts for information.

MARKET RESEARCH TEXTS:

Cheap But Good Marketing Research
Alan Andreasen
Irwin Professional Publishing
1991

Do It Yourself Marketing Research
George Breen and
A.B. Blankenship
McGraw-Hill, 1992

Marketing on a Shoestring: Low-Cost Tips for Marketing Your Products or Services
Jeffrey P. Davidson
John Wiley and Sons, 1988

The New Marketing Research Systems: How to Use Strategic Database Information for Better Marketing Decisions
David J. Curry
Wiley, 1992

COMPETITIVE INTELLIGENCE:

Advances in Competitive Intelligence
John E. Prescott
University of Pittsburgh Press, 1989

Analyzing Your Competition
FIND/SVP, 1991

The Business Intelligence System
Benjamin and Tamar Gilad
AMACOM Publications, 1988

Competitor Intelligence Manual & Guide
Kirk Tyson
Kirk Tyson, 1990

How to Analyze the Competition
Lorna M. Daniells, et al
Washington Researchers, 1993

How to Find Information About Companies
Lorna M. Daniells, et al
Washington Researchers, 1993

Monitoring the Competition
Leonard M. Fuld
John Wiley and Sons, 1988

The New Competitor Intelligence: The Complete Resource for Finding,

Analyzing, & Using Information about Your Competitors
Leonard M. Fuld
Wiley, 1994

Outsmarting the Competition
John J. McGonagle, Jr. and
Carolyn M. Vella
McGraw-Hill, 1993

Two other excellent books that don't quite fit under the above categories, but provide very timely advice in how to use information for strategic business advantage are *Competing for the Future* by Gary Hamel and C.K. Prahalad (Harvard Business Press, 1994) and *Jumping the Curve: Innovation and Strategic Choice in an Age of Transition,* by Nicholas Imparto and Oren Harari (Jossey-Bass, 1994)

Appendix VI

Guides to Organizing an Information-Finding System

If you want to establish a library or information center, there are several sources you can turn to. The first two guides listed here are published by the leading association of business and institutional libraries, the Special Libraries Association.

Special Libraries: Increasing the Information Edge (1993)
Special Libraries Association
1700 18th Street NW
Washington DC 20009
(202) 234-4700

Special Libraries and Information Centers: An Introductory Text, 3rd Edition (1995)
Special Libraries Association
1700 18th Street NW
Washington, DC 20009
(202) 234-4700

Another book, published by Find/SVP, is a professional advancement guidebook which analyzes how technology and broad business trends are changing the role of the company information center. It offers advice to business librarians and information specialists on how they can insure that they remain a valuable strategic asset to their organization:

Rethinking the Corporate Information Center (1995)
FIND/SVP
625 Avenue of the Americas
New York, NY 10011
(212) 645-4500

Finally, the two organizations listed below can be of assistance in creating your own in-house business information center.

American Library Association
50 East Huron Street
Chicago, IL 60611
(312) 944-6780

This association can be of assistance in establishing a library. ALA also publishes a book called Managing Small Library Collections in Business and Community Organizations (1989).

American Society for
Information Science
8720 Georgia Avenue
Suite 501
Silver Spring, MD 20910-3602
(301) 495-0900

This is another helpful association in the field of information science.

Two other professional associations that may be helpful are the Information Industry Association, located in Washington, DC (202-639-8260), and The Society of Competitive Intelligence Professionals (SCIP) 818 18th St. NW, No. 225,Washington, DC 20006 (202)223-5885.

You can keep track of new business information sources and developments in the information industry by subscribing to one of several magazines and newsletters that cover this field. These include publications from the Special Libraries Association (Washington DC), such as *SpeciaList* which is of particular interest to librarians; *The Information Report* from Washington Researchers (Washington DC), geared mostly to identifying sources of competitor intelligence; and *The Information Advisor*, published by our firm, FIND/SVP (New York City) which compares competing sources of business information and advises how to perform quality and cost effective research.

Appendix VII

A Generalist's Source List

This might seem crazy to any information specialist worth his or her salt, but in this appendix we're going to try to give you a brief list of sources and services that should be familiar to every business generalist.

Our generalist's source list begins with all the previous appendices. It continues with the following annotated list of items and organizations that should be found in any business library, and that every executive should be familiar with. Note that today many of these sources can be found online.

The Census Catalog & Guide, published by the Bureau of the Census, and available from the United States Government Printing Office, is a must, containing a descriptive list of all products and services available from the Census. Don't forget to subscribe to two other essential United States government publications: *County Business Patterns* and the *Survey of Current Business*. The former lists employment and payroll statistics, broken down by county, while the latter provides broader aggregate estimates and analyses of United States economic activity as a whole.

The American Statistics Index, published by the Congressional Information Service, is a comprehensive guide to the statistical publications of the United States government.

If you really want to keep up with who the real experts are behind these federal government sources, you should probably buy a copy of *Who Knows: A Guide to Washington Experts*, a paperback directory published by Washington Researchers that identifies and provides contact information for thousands of experts in Washington.

For recent financial statements and other information on publicly-held companies, everyone should have either or both *Moody's Manuals* (Moody's Investors Services) and *Standard & Poors Corporation Records* (Standard and Poors). To determine industry ratio norms, you can check either *The Almanac of Business and Industry Financial Ratios*, which lists 50 performance indicators derived from tax return filings from 37 million corporations or *Dun & Bradstreet's Industry Norms & Key Business Ratios*, derived from one million financial statements filed with D&B.

For general information on various industries, there are *Standard and Poors Industry Surveys* and the annual *U.S. Industrial Outlook*, published by the United States Department of Commerce.

To discover a company's divisions and subsidiaries, you should have access to *America's Corporate Families*, published by Dun's Marketing Services; it lists over 4,000 parent companies around the world and nearly 20,000 subsidiaries. Two other top guides for locating subsidiaries and divisions are *Who Owns Whom* (Dun & Bradstreet) and the *Directory of Corporate Affiliations* (Reed Reference Publishing).

Another excellent Dun's directory, this one for finding facts on overseas firms, is *Principal International Businesses*. It lists key facts for over 50,000 firms in 113 countries.

Other guides to international business you should be familiar with include *How to Find Information About Foreign Firms*, published by Washington Researchers, and the series of marketing directories published by the London-based EuroMonitor. You can keep up with what the European Community is publishing by getting a catalogue from an organization in Lanham, Maryland called UNIPUB.

The *Survey of Buying Power* and the *Survey of Industrial Purchasing Power* are two special issues of *Sales and Marketing Management* magazine that should be on every marketing person's shelf. Another key directory covering the marketing field is the *International Directory of Market Research Houses and Services*, published by the American Marketing Association.

Basic international data can be found in the United Nation's *Statistical Yearbook* and *Demographic Yearbook*. No one can do without Dun & Bradstreet's *Million Dollar Directory*, which provides basic information on 50,000 companies. To be included, companies must either have 250 or more employees, or sales of over $25 million. Another key company directory is Standard & Poor's *Register of Corporations, Directors & Executives*, which includes information on about 55,000 companies. If you need to keep track of high technology firms, a very useful directory is the *CorpTech Directory of Technology Companies*, which provides data on 40,000 high tech firms.

Finally, a less expensive company directory you may want to check out is *Hoover's Handbook* (The Reference Press, Austin, TX). This handbook (which publishes separate United States and world directories) covers only the very largest companies, and is much less comprehensive than the other directories. However, it does provide more details on those firms it does cover, and is a *significantly* less expensive purchase.

Dun's Business Rankings and *Ward's Business Directory* list companies according to their SIC codes and sales. Private as well as public companies are included. An easy way to look up all sorts of rankings is through the very useful *Business Rankings Annual*, which ranks the top ten firms for thousands of industries and categories. The data is compiled by the Brooklyn, New York Business Library, and the book is published by Gale Research.

The *Standard Directory of Advertisers*, and its companion, the *Directory of Advertising Agencies*, published by the National Register Publishing Company, contain thousands of names of key executives at companies that advertise, as well as their agencies.

The *Thomas Register of American Manufacturers* and the *Thomas Register Catalog File* (Thomas Publishing Company) is a multi-volume set that lists virtually all United States manufacturers of any significance, alphabetically and by product, and also contains reproductions of product catalogs.

The *Dun & Bradstreet Reference Book* is probably the most complete published list of companies and includes their principal SIC number and estimated financial strength rating.

Business Publication Rates and Data, published by the Standard Rate and Data Service, contains a wealth of information on all business publications. Standard Rate and Data also publishes similar directories covering consumer publications, other media and direct mail lists. The entire set should be in every business library. *Who's Who In America* is published by Marquis Who's Who, which also has companion directories (e.g., *Who's Who in the East, Who's Who of American Women*, etc.).

State Industrial Directories, which describe business and economic activity within a particular state, are available from various sources, including State Economic Development offices, chambers of commerces, and private publishers.

The *Statistical Abstract of the United States*, published by the United States Bureau of the Census, is an information "Bible" that includes a wealth of industrial, social, political, and economic statistics; as is the *Information Please Almanac*, published annually by Houghton Mifflin.

No one should forget these two reference basics: the new *Encyclopedia Brittanica* and Webster's *Third New International Dictionary of the English Language*.

The index to articles in business periodicals is the *Business Periodicals Index*, published by H.W. Wilson. The published index to articles in general and non-technical publications is the *Reader's Guide to Periodical Literature*, also published by H.W. Wilson.

The index to current information on companies and industries is the *F&S Index of Corporations & Industries*, produced by Predicasts, Inc. In fact, Predicasts has so many other important information services and products that you should request its brochures for your files immediately.

A *Statistics Sources* (Gale Research Company) is a good subject guide to data on industrial, business, social, educational, financial, and other topics.

Newsletters in Print, also published by Gale, provides a list of newsletters in thousands of subject fields.

While you're at it, get a catalog of the directories and publications of Gale Research Inc. (Detroit, MI), as they are probably the leading business reference publisher in the country, and have a variety of very useful books and publications.

In case this isn't already obvious, every business should subscribe to *Business Week, Forbes, Fortune*, and the *Harvard Business Review* as well as *The New York Times* and *The Wall Street Journal*. Beyond that, your own specific field will determine which periodicals you should read regularly. Smaller companies should subscribe to *Inc.* Executives anxious to keep up should read *Bottom Line Business*. And every business should make sure it receives the leading trade journals in its field. To find out what these are, check the *Gale Directory of Publications and Broadcast Media*, or one of the other periodical directories.

About the Authors

Andrew P. Garvin is president of FIND/SVP, Inc., a leading New York-based consulting, research, and knowledge-gathering service.

Cofounded by Mr. Garvin in 1969, FIND/SVP is part of the worldwide network of SVP consulting and information services. FIND/SVP pioneered the concept of providing research and consulting services by telephone in the United States, and now serves the research needs of over 2,300 organizations. It also publishes and distributes a variety of market reports, newsletters, and information products. In 1974, FIND/SVP's Quick Information Service won the Information Industry Association's Product-of-the-Year Award.

From 1979 to 1982, Mr. Garvin was a member of the board of directors of the Information Industry Association and was chairman of the 1979 National Information Conference and Exposition. He remains active in the association. Since 1987, he has been a member of the Young Presidents' Organization. Prior to starting FIND/SVP, Mr. Garvin was vice president of his own public relations and marketing firm, and earlier was a correspondent for *Newsweek*.

A frequent speaker on information-related topics, Mr.

Garvin holds a BA in political science from Yale University and an MS in journalism from the Columbia School of Journalism. He lives in New York City with his wife, daughter, and son.

Robert Berkman has spent over fifteen years in the information business. After graduating from the University of Virginia in 1980, he joined McGraw-Hill Inc. in New York City and worked as a senior editor until 1986. In 1987 he wrote *Find It Fast: How to Uncover Expert Information on Any Subject*, which was published by HarperCollins and revised in 1994. Other books include *Find it Online!* (McGraw-Hill, 1994) and *Rethinking the Corporate Information Center* (Find/SVP, 1995). Mr. Berkman spent two years living in Missoula, Montana, where he received his M.A. in journalism from the University of Montana and taught a course there in online database research. Berkman is the editor of *The Information Advisor*, an international monthly newsletter for business researchers. He currently lives in Washington DC, with his wife and stepdaughter.

Index